Humanitarian Journalists

This book documents the unique reporting practices of humanitarian journalists – an influential group of journalists defying conventional approaches to covering humanitarian crises.

Based on a 5-year study, involving over 150 in-depth interviews, this book examines the political, economic and social forces that sustain and influence humanitarian journalists. The authors argue that – by amplifying marginalised voices and providing critical, in-depth explanations of neglected crises – these journalists show us that another kind of humanitarian journalism is possible. However, the authors also reveal the heavy price these reporters pay for deviating from conventional journalistic norms. Their peripheral position at the 'boundary zone' between the journalistic and humanitarian fields means that a humanitarian journalist's job is often precarious – with direct implications for their work, especially as 'watchdogs' for the aid sector. As a result, they urgently need more support if they are to continue to do this work and promote more effective and accountable humanitarian action.

A rigorous study of how unique professional practices can be produced at the 'boundary zone' between fields, this book will interest students and scholars of journalism and communication studies, sociology and humanitarian studies. It will also appeal to those interested in studies of news and media work as occupational identities.

Martin Scott is an Associate Professor in Media and International Development at the University of East Anglia.

Kate Wright is a Senior Lecturer in Media and Communications, Politics, and International Relations at the University of Edinburgh.

Mel Bunce is a Professor of International Journalism and Head of the Journalism Department at City, University of London.

Routledge Focus on Journalism Studies

Australian Sports Journalism
Power, Control and Threats
Peter English

When Media Succumbs to Rising Authoritarianism
Cautionary Tales from Venezuela's Recent History
Edited by Ezequiel Korin and Paromita Pain

Front-Page Scotland
Newspapers and the Scottish Independence Referendum
David Patrick

Public Television in Poland
Political Pressure and Public Service Media in a Post-communist
Country
Agnieszka Węglińska

Election Politics and the Mass Press in Long Edwardian Britain
Christopher Shoop-Worrall

Journalism's Racial Reckoning
The News Media's Pivot to Diversity and Inclusion
Brad Clark

Re-examining the UK Newspaper Industry
Marc Edge

Humanitarian Journalists
Covering Crises from a Boundary Zone
Martin Scott, Kate Wright, and Mel Bunce

Humanitarian Journalists

Covering Crises from a
Boundary Zone

**Martin Scott, Kate Wright, and
Mel Bunce**

Routledge
Taylor & Francis Group

LONDON AND NEW YORK

First published 2023
by Routledge
4 Park Square, Milton Park, Abingdon, Oxon OX14 4RN

and by Routledge
605 Third Avenue, New York, NY 10158

Routledge is an imprint of the Taylor & Francis Group, an informa business

British Library Cataloguing-in-Publication Data
A catalogue record for this book is available from the British Library

ISBN: 978-1-032-40767-8 (hbk)
ISBN: 978-1-032-41207-8 (pbk)
ISBN: 978-1-003-35680-6 (ebk)

DOI: 10.4324/9781003356806

Typeset in Times New Roman
by codeMantra

Rucke Souza / Cartoon Movement.

Contents

Figures

Tables

Preface

Sophia[1] is a humanitarian journalist. She works for a small non-profit news outlet that covers international aid and global affairs. She regularly reports on under-reported crises, with a focus on in-depth, explanatory and solutions-oriented journalism. She is particularly keen to highlight the perspective not only of affected citizens but also of a range of other local actors including rebels, aid workers, politicians and think-tanks. She has significant freedom to choose which stories to cover and how to report them and regularly commissions local stringers living in affected countries.

Sophia used to work for a large international news broadcaster. Despite having a permanent position and a significantly higher salary, she left after just 18 months because she was frustrated by what she felt was their rigid and formulaic approach to covering global affairs. She thought that much of their coverage of recent humanitarian crises was superficial and fleeting. Although she was proud that she helped to break a news story revealing corruption within an international NGO, she worries that it unfairly damaged the reputation of the humanitarian sector as a whole, because some of the subtleties of international humanitarian response got lost in the reporting.

The news organisation Sophia works for now generates very little advertising or reader revenue and relies almost exclusively on short-term grant funding from a very small number of private foundations. Although she has never felt under any pressure to cover stories in ways that might please their current or potential donors, she does resent the amount of time it takes to meet their reporting requirements. If their funding is cut, and she loses her job, she intends to work either as a freelance journalist or as an aid agency press officer. The only other news outlet she is aware of that covers similar stories has recently closed due to a lack of funding.

Sophia has never actually met any of her current colleagues in person as they all work remotely, in different countries. During their daily online editorial meetings they frequently disagree about which stories fall within their remit. There is no consensus about what makes a story 'humanitarian', as opposed to a human rights or global development issue, for example. For this reason, some of the stories she pitches still get rejected – and she doesn't fully understand why.

Although Sophia was recently nominated for a One World Media award, in general, she is frustrated by the lack of recognition and reach of her work. She also worries about being able to pay the bills – she knows her job is precarious. But despite this lack of external recognition and the financial risks, Sophia is glad she took this job – because it allows her the freedom to do the kind of work she has always wanted to do.

Sophia is one of a small group of 'humanitarian journalists' whose work bridges the worlds of international news production and humanitarianism. She is motivated by both the traditional journalistic desire to document, witness and explain events and the desire to help alleviate suffering and save lives. There are a small number of news outlets employing humanitarian journalists like Sophia, who play a valuable role in the global media system. This book is about those individuals. It seeks to describe, explain and evaluate their work.

Note

1 'Sophia' is a fictional journalist, constructed in ways which illustrate key themes in our findings (see Kotišová 2019 for an illustration of how creative non-fiction can be used to study crisis reporting).

Acknowledgements

The idea for this book originated on Thursday 27 March 2014, when we saw an online petition urging then UN Secretary General Ban Ki-moon to 'Save IRIN, a UN-established, award-winning Africa-based news network' (Francesca 2014). According to the petition, journalists at IRIN (which later became The New Humanitarian) produced 'vital... humanitarian journalism' on a 'microscopic budget' using their 'unique skills and access', at a time of 'unprecedented political upheavals and conflict'. Despite this, 'IRIN's parent organization in the UN has decided to wind it down'.

This immediately prompted a range of questions, not only about why the UN was 'shut[ting] it down' – but more broadly about what 'unique skills' IRIN's journalists might have and how their reporting might differ from more conventional news coverage of humanitarian affairs? What other, similar sources of 'humanitarian reporting' might there be, if any? In short, who are humanitarian journalists? We were only able to begin answering these questions because the senior management of IRIN at the time – Ben Parker and Heba Aly – agreed to let us observe and interview their staff, as they transitioned away from the UN.

Since then, over 150 people have agreed to be interviewed for this research. This includes representatives of UN agencies, governmental and philanthropic donors, INGOs and intermediary organisations, as well as journalists working for Agence France-Presse (AFP), Al Jazeera English, Associated Press, BBC World Service, the BBC, BRIGHT Magazine, Buzzfeed, CGTN, Channel 4 News, CNN, Devex, El Pais, Goats and Soda (NPR), The Guardian, HumAngle, Humanosphere, India Blooms, Inter Press Service, the International Consortium of Investigative Journalists, ITN, Just Earth News, the New York Times, News Deeply, Nuba Reports, PassBlue, Pro Publica, ReliefWeb, Reuters, SciDev.Net, Sky News, The New Humanitarian (formerly IRIN), the Thomson Reuters Foundation, UN Dispatch, Vice News, Voice of America, Washington Post, World Post and Xinhua. We are extremely grateful to all of our interviewees for how generously they shared their time, thoughts and experiences.

We are also grateful to those who have supported us in other aspects of this research including research assistants Jessie Hagen and Fiona Elliot, mentors Dan Brockington and Sally-Ann Wilson, transcriber Georgie Aronin, designer Emma Bailey and our Commissioning Editor at Routledge Suzanne Richardson. We also wish to thank those who have given us feedback on the ideas discussed in this book including Alexandra Budabin, Lilie Chouliaraki, Florencia Enghel, Alice Fenyoe, Jonathan Ong, Shani Orgad, Lisa Ann Richey, Alexa Robertson, Ludek Stavinoha and Nikki Usher – who first introduced us to the work of Gil Eyal and Grace Pok. Thanks also to Monika Krause and Peter English for giving us permission to reproduce their Figures in this book.

This book is one part of our wider Humanitarian Journalism Research Project, which was initially supported by a grant from the UK Arts and Humanities Research Council (grant number AH/N00731X/1). Since then, our research has also been supported by the Independent Social Research Foundation (ISRF), as well as by institutional funding from our respective universities – the University of East Anglia (UEA), the University of Edinburgh and City, University of London. All our publications from this wider research project are available open access and can be found at humanitarian-journalism.net.

Finally, as always, we are grateful to our friends and families for their support and patience. Since we began this project, working conditions in Higher Education have deteriorated, making long-term collaborative research projects increasingly challenging. These difficulties were further compounded by the effects of the Covid pandemic. Given this, the support of our friends, families and colleagues has been invaluable. Thank you.

Abbreviations

AFP	Agence France Presse
AP	Associated Press
BBC	British Broadcasting Corporation
CGTN	China Global Television Network News
DAC	Development Assistance Committee
FTS	Financial Tracking Service
ICRC	International Committee of the Red Cross
INGO	International non-governmental organisation
IPCC	Intergovernmental Panel on Climate Change
IRIN	Integrated Regional Information Networks (now The New Humanitarian)
MSF	Médecins Sans Frontières
NGO	Non-Governmental Organisation
NPR	National Public Radio
NWICO	New World Information and Communication Order
TNH	The New Humanitarian
UN	United Nations
UNESCO	United Nations Educational, Scientific and Cultural Organization
UNOCHA	United Nations Office for the Coordination of Humanitarian Affairs

Introduction

Who are humanitarian journalists?

Prior to the 2022 Russian invasion of Ukraine, the armed conflict in the Donetsk and Luhansk regions was the second most under-reported humanitarian crisis in the world (see Figure 0.1). In 2021, it was the subject of just 801 online news articles globally, out of over 1.8 million articles analysed by Care International (2022).[1] In 2020, it received even less media attention – just 702 articles (Care International 2021). During this time, around 3.4 million people in eastern Ukraine needed humanitarian assistance, including 1.3 million elderly people (OCHA 2022).

Other consistently 'forgotten' crises include the 1.2 million people in Zambia experiencing acute levels of food insecurity, which received

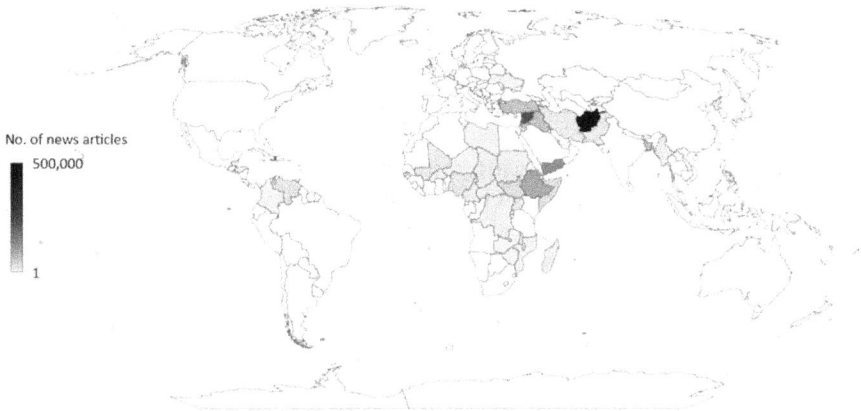

No. of news articles
500,000

1

Figure 0.1 Volume of online news coverage of the 40 largest humanitarian crises in 2021.

Source: Data provided by Care International and Meltwater. See Chapter Notes for a full list of data.

DOI: 10.4324/9781003356806-1

just 512 online news reports in 2021; and the 2.8 million people in need of humanitarian aid in Honduras, because of chronic poverty and violence, which received just 3,920 online news articles in 2021 (Care International 2022). To put these figures in context, during the same period, there were 91,979 online articles globally about the announcement that actors Ben Affleck and Jennifer Lopez were dating again, and 239,422 news articles about billionaires Jeff Bezos and Elon Musk taking space flights (ibid).

However, not all humanitarian crises are 'forgotten'. Figure 0.1 also shows that a small number receive considerably more attention than most others. For example, in 2021, the humanitarian crisis in Afghanistan was the subject of nearly half a million (475,744) online news items – more than 33 other crises combined. Similarly, in 2022, the war in Ukraine drew a vast amount of international media attention. At its peak, it was the subject of 35% of all online global news coverage (see Alexander and Rozzell 2022).

Such extreme disparities in media attention are a longstanding and well-documented feature of international news coverage and the result of conventional journalistic norms and practices, as well as structural influences. Research has repeatedly demonstrated that the volume of international news coverage a humanitarian crisis receives is primarily a reflection of its geo-political significance and its resonance with journalistic news values – rather than the number of people affected (Kwak and An 2014; Yan and Bissell 2015). Adams (1986:113), for example, found that 'the severity of foreign natural disasters explains less than 10% of the variation in the amount of attention they are given in nightly U.S. television newscasts'. Instead, as Franks (2006:284) put it, 'Western self-interest is the precondition for significant coverage of a humanitarian crisis'.

These disparities in media attention – and this disconnect with levels of suffering – have important consequences. They can compound the limited international political attention that most crises receive, because politicians are under less pressure to act (Hawkins 2011; Brommesson and Ekengren 2017). The under-reporting of humanitarian crises can also exacerbate disparities in the amount of funding they receive from international donors (Cohen, Riffe and Kim 2021). For example, our own research recently demonstrated that a large amount of sudden-onset, national news coverage can pressure governments to allocate greater support to a humanitarian crisis – even if the level of unmet need does not require it (Scott, Bunce and Wright 2022).

More broadly, these acute disparities in media attention reproduce a 'hierarchy of human life' in which some people's lives are represented as more worthy of attention than others, which ultimately helps to fuel prejudice and injustices (Chouliaraki 2006; Joye 2009). For instance, in May 2022, while 91% of UK adults were aware of the war in Ukraine, just 23% were aware of the humanitarian crisis in the Horn of Africa, which was affecting almost 20 million people (Davies 2022).

But the episodic and selective nature of conventional news coverage of humanitarian crises is only one part of a bigger and largely untold story about the relationship between journalism and humanitarianism. In this book, we show that there are a small but influential number of *humanitarian* journalists who defy many conventional journalistic norms. These humanitarian journalists work largely for specialist international news outlets such as Devex, HumAngle, India Blooms, Inter Press Service, Just Earth News, SciDev.Net, The New Humanitarian (formerly IRIN) and UN Dispatch.

In contrast to more conventional journalists, their professional practices are informed by hybrid combinations of journalistic and humanitarian principles. For example, their strong adherence to the humanitarian norm of 'moral equivalence' – the idea that all lives have equal worth – means that they continue to cover humanitarian crises even when these do not correspond with conventional news values. For instance, in 2021, when eastern Ukraine was almost entirely overlooked by most news outlets, The New Humanitarian continued to publish in-depth stories about the impact of the Covid pandemic on the conflict (Sopova and Taylor-Lind 2021), for example, and the inadequacies of mental health support for children affected by the war (Laichter 2021). Similarly, after the Russian invasion in 2022, when global media attention focused heavily on Ukraine, humanitarian journalists continued covering other 'forgotten' crises in Malawi, Guatemala, Burundi, Niger, Zimbabwe and elsewhere, which conventional news outlets were largely ignoring.

But reporting under-reported crises is not the only way humanitarian journalists' professional practices differ from conventional journalism. We also show that the format of and sourcing practices within their coverage is distinct. Their adherence to the humanitarian principle of 'moral equivalence' leads them to amplify marginalised voices connected to humanitarian crises, such as affected citizens and local volunteers. For example, The New Humanitarian's article about children's mental health in eastern Ukraine in 2021 focused primarily on the testimonies of children themselves, along with their guardians, parents and grandparents (Laichter 2021).

By contrast, Lawson (2021) has shown that within conventional news coverage of humanitarian crises, there is an especially heavy reliance on a narrow range of institutional sources, such as the United Nations and large INGOs. This reliance on a 'hierarchy of trustworthy sources' (Lawson 2021:1) enables journalists to maintain the credibility of their work without the need to verify, contest and/or challenge the official information they cite. However, it also means that the international institutions they 'hide behind' (ibid) routinely become the 'primary definers' (Hall et al. 1978) of a crisis – that is, experts who have the power to frame and interpret events for the audience.

Such an approach is problematic because it often leads to coverage which emphasises the agency of international rescue efforts at the expense of affected communities and local response teams. It can also inhibit critical assessments of the international response and foreclose discussion of alternatives to humanitarian action, or alternative understandings of 'humanitarianism' itself (Hopgood 2008). In short, it can reproduce an apolitical view of humanitarian crises. For example, in their analysis of Spanish press coverage of the Darfur conflict, Gutiérrez and García (2011) conclude that reporting not only privileged the perspective of European humanitarian organisations, but also drew attention to the consequences of events rather their causes, and presented Dafuris as playing a passive and secondary role.

In addition to 'reporting under-reported crises' and 'amplifying marginalised voices', humanitarian journalists seek to 'add value' to mainstream news coverage of humanitarian crises – in accordance with the humanitarian principle of 'making the most difference' (Krause 2014). This is usually achieved by providing longer-form, explanatory journalism and/or by experimenting with different formats. For example, in its coverage of humanitarian issues in Africa, HumAngle regularly makes use of infographics, cartoon illustrations, Twitter Space discussions, geospatial tools, explainer videos, documentaries, interactive dashboards and weekly podcasts. Humanitarian journalists are also often able to 'add value' through their reporting because they operate with a more informed understanding of humanitarian principles and the aid sector and have a more collaborative and outcome-oriented approach to their work. This often leads them to adopt the role of a constructive watchdog for the aid sector. For example, HumAngle recently collaborated with the Premium Times Centre for Investigative Journalism (PTCIJ) on a series of stories that uncovered corruption in the management of displaced people in Northeast Nigeria.

By contrast, previous research has consistently concluded that conventional news coverage of humanitarian crises frequently adopts the same 'standard characteristics' (Bacon and Nash 2004:19), and 'ubiquitous... humanitarian imaginary' (Stupart 2022:221). The main features of this 'template' of conventional humanitarian reporting are well characterised by Ardèvol-Abreu (2016) who, in a study of Spanish press coverage of humanitarian crises, identified four dominant news frames – war, violence, Islamic terrorism and crime. Ardèvol-Abreu (2016:49) also found that, despite their different editorial viewpoints, the use of these dominant frames showed 'very little variation' amongst the four newspapers studied. Ultimately, Ardèvol-Abreu (2016) concluded that there is a dominant macro-frame of Spanish press coverage of humanitarian crisis which characterises such events as a threat to the 'North', produced by corruption, terrorism and political incompetence, which can only be resolved either by foreign military force or humanitarian assistance. Research shows that the repeated use of this dominant frame leads audiences to instinctively dismiss or actively avoid news coverage about distant suffering (Cohen 2001; VSO 2001; Scott 2018; Seu and Orgad 2017).

Despite its limitations, conventional journalistic approaches to covering humanitarian crises can still serve some important normative goals. They can increase international awareness and even charitable donations from the public for a small number of crises. For instance, in their study of media influence on charitable giving after the 2004 Indian Ocean earthquake and tsunami, Brown and Minty (2006) found that an additional minute of nightly news coverage or an additional story in a major newspaper raised donations by between 17% and 21%, even when controlling for timings and tax considerations. Similarly, van Belle, Rioux and Potter (2004:134) found that one story about a foreign disaster in the New York Times is associated with an increase of more than US$375,000 in US foreign disaster assistance – even when its severity has been taken into account. Furthermore, Cooper (2020:747) has shown that legacy media were central to ensuring that the 2018 sexual abuse scandals concerning Oxfam GB and Save the Children UK – which had been known about for some years within the aid sector – finally received widespread attention.

Given this, we contend that conventional journalistic approaches are not inherently problematic, but that they can become so if they are the only way in which humanitarian affairs are reported. The contrasting coverage produced by humanitarian journalists therefore provides a valuable addition – especially at a time when a diverse range of critical and informed coverage of humanitarian affairs has never been more important. Climate change is causing widespread disruption in nature, affecting the lives of billions of people around the world.

Increased heatwaves, droughts and floods, for example, are exposing millions more people to acute food and water insecurity (IPCC 2022). In addition, the escalating and interacting impacts of biodiversity loss, forced migrations, increasingly protracted conflicts and global pandemics are collectively fuelling rapid increases in humanitarian need around the world.

In 2022, the UN requested $41 billion to help 183 million people in need across 63 countries – nearly double the amount requested in 2019, and three times the number of people in need than in 2015 (Alexander 2022; OCHA 2022). This expansion in humanitarian need is far outstripping levels of international humanitarian support – which is largely flatlining. In 2021, the gap between requirements and funding was the second largest ever, with the UN's humanitarian response plans and appeals only 54% funded (FTS 2021). In this context, it is essential that journalism helps to support more effective, needs-based and accountable responses to humanitarian crises.

Despite producing valuable content, humanitarian journalists pay a heavy price for deviating from conventional journalistic norms. In this book, we also show that they occupy a peripheral position in both the journalistic and humanitarian fields and, as a result, they often suffer from a lack of recognition and financial security. This has direct implications for their work, especially their ability to act as 'watchdogs' of the aid sector. For this reason, we argue that humanitarian journalists need far greater support – but we caution against interventions which could compromise their unique journalistic-humanitarian values.

We also argue that humanitarian journalists help to challenge some of our longstanding assumptions about news coverage of humanitarian affairs. They demonstrate that the episodic, simplistic and selective nature of much news coverage of humanitarian crises is not inevitable. There is nothing intrinsically 'un-newsworthy' about humanitarian crises like those currently occurring in South Sudan, Somalia and Yemen. News values are socially constructed and while dominant interpretations of these values are often reproduced by news producers, we show that they are also routinely modified, adapted and challenged by others. In short, the news producers we study in this book show that another kind of humanitarian journalism is possible.

This critical review of the norms and values of humanitarian journalists also gives us an opportunity to re-think how professional fields in general constrain and enable different forms of practice. Throughout this book, we demonstrate that the practices of the humanitarian journalists in our study are an outcome of their social positioning vis-à-vis the fields of 'journalism' and 'humanitarianism'. Specifically, we show that they are neither fully inside nor outside either field, but situated at the 'thick boundary zone' (Eyal 2013:170) between them. Following Eyal (2013:180), we show that this is an under-regulated 'space of opportunity' – characterised by ambiguity – which enables new forms of hybrid practice to emerge, as the norms and values from multiple fields meet.

This book also speaks to conversations about why journalists choose to engage in journalism, despite its rapidly decreasing symbolic and material rewards (Powers and Vera-Sembrano, forthcoming), and why some journalists choose to pursue particularly precarious, or poorly paid forms of reporting, in order to represent the suffering of others (Stupart 2020, 2021a, 2021b). Powers and Vera-Sembrano (forthcoming) outline various 'modes of adjustment' journalists engage in to hold onto what Bourdieu (1993) would call *illusio* – that sense of why 'the game of journalism' is worth playing. We show that humanitarian journalists engage in a different 'mode of adjustment': trading in the symbolic or material capital they previously held within the journalistic or humanitarian fields, to have the freedom to produce the kinds of specialist reporting they enjoy, value and care passionately about in the 'thick boundary zone' between these fields.

Finally, we contribute to what Ferron, Kotišová and Smith (2022:3) describe as a 'recent trend not to grant epistemic privilege to the mainstream news media, professional elites and their dominant meta-discourse and instead to investigate overlooked sub-groups and practice'. The world's communications ecologies are rapidly changing and diversifying in response to economic and technological disruption, and the arrival of non-traditional actors including NGOs and citizens who make news content and, in doing so, blur the boundaries of who and what constitutes journalism. It is therefore important not to assume that the most significant professional practices are always those that have been firmly institutionalised (see Deuze and Witschge 2017). In particular, our research suggests that we might begin to consider journalistic 'beats' – not simply as thematically-defined subject areas of news coverage, but as potential 'boundary zones' between the journalistic and non-journalistic fields, where other potentially valuable, hybrid professional practices may be emerging. This might be equally true, for example, of other specialist areas such as business journalism or sports journalism.

In the remainder of this opening chapter, we explain who these humanitarian journalists are, and how we identified them and studied their practices, before giving a more detailed overview of the different chapters in this book.

Finding humanitarian journalists

Identifying alternative ways of reporting humanitarian affairs – and the individuals and organisations who practice them – is surprisingly difficult. When we started this study in 2015, very few news outlets publicly identified themselves or their content as 'humanitarian'. Furthermore, we wanted to avoid imposing our own definition of what 'counts' as humanitarian journalism because this might exclude some important practices, as well as risking ethnocentricity. We were acutely aware that the term 'humanitarian' is not only a 'contested terrain', but also something of a 'sticky signifier, capable of holding on simultaneously to multiple discourses and meanings' (Cottle and Cooper 2019:2). For example, there are longstanding tensions between the 'chemical' strand of humanitarianism, which seeks only to provide immediate relief to those who are suffering; and the 'alchemical' strand, which also tries to prevent suffering by challenging its structural causes of suffering (Barnett 2011; Orgad 2013). Moreover, we are mindful that the practice of calling oneself a 'humanitarian journalist' is, as we explain in more detail later, 'rarely a neutral act of self-description. It is also a strategic move in a social game' (Medvetz 2012:34).

We began this study, therefore, by casting a very wide net. In 2016, we commissioned the media monitoring service – Kantar – to carry out digital keyword searches of over 20,000 English-language news outlets, to identify all those that reported on four different 'humanitarian' events or issues. These events included a rapid-onset disaster (an earthquake), a UN appeal for humanitarian funding for multiple crises, a long-running and highly complex conflict (in South Sudan) and the first Global Humanitarian Summit, which focused on aid policy.[2]

We found that only 12 news outlets – or 0.0006% of the sample – covered all four events. As expected, this included major international news agencies such as Agence France Presse (AFP), Associated Press (AP), Thomson Reuters and the Xinhua News Agency – which many local and national news outlets rely on for their international reporting (Palmer 2019). Four of the largest international broadcasters also covered all four events, including Al Jazeera English, the BBC World Service, China Global Television Network news (CGTN) and Voice of America. So too did two relatively small, non-profit international news outlets – The New Humanitarian and Humanosphere.[3]

We began interviewing journalists from all 12 organisations and continued 'snowballing' to identify further journalists around the world who frequently reported internationally on humanitarian affairs. In total, we interviewed over 120 practicing journalists from 37 different news outlets between 2016 and 2020. During this time, we also interviewed 30 representatives of UN agencies, governmental and philanthropic donors, INGOs and intermediary organisations. In semi-structured interviews, we asked journalists about their news values, professional role perceptions, daily practices and how they related to those they reported on, their editors, audiences and funders. Many of these individuals shared the same, conventional journalistic norms and practices, and produced the kinds of conventional reporting on humanitarian crises that has been well documented in previous research, which we described above.

But crucially – and fascinatingly – we identified within this larger sample a significant number of individuals whose professional norms and practices consistently defied conventional journalistic norms. This smaller group of approximately 30 journalists are the primary focus of this book. These individuals worked primarily for international, online, non-profit news outlets – though many also work or have worked as freelancers. Few were employed by commercial, state, or public service news outlets. These specialist news organisations included BRIGHT Magazine, Devex, Goats and Soda (NPR), Humanosphere, HumAngle, India Blooms, Inter Press Service, Just Earth News, News Deeply, PassBlue, SciDev.Net, The New Humanitarian (formerly IRIN), UN Dispatch and WorldPost – though several of these outlets have since closed.

Despite having a much smaller reach than national and international broadcasters, these specialist news outlets are still highly influential. Those which directly target professionals working in the aid sector – such as Devex and The New Humanitarian – are heavily relied upon by this community for specialist information, analysis and investigations. Indeed, our survey of aid worker attitudes towards the media[4] – which we cite throughout the book – showed that 39% of The New Humanitarian's readers regard its journalism is 'extremely' or 'very important' to their work. Several of these organisations are also attached to larger news outlets, which syndicate their content to a much wider audience, such as Goats and Soda (NPR).

These specialist news outlets are also important because they tend to cover humanitarian affairs differently to national media and international broadcasters. We illustrate this point throughout the book, by drawing on the results of two separate content analyses: a study of news coverage of the 2015 Nepal earthquake by Reuters and The New Humanitarian,[5] and an analysis of news coverage of humanitarian crises in Yemen and South Sudan in 2017 by Al Jazeera English, the BBC World Service, CGTN (Africa and Americas), CNN International, the Mail Online, Devex, The Guardian, The New Humanitarian and The Washington Post.[6] In our study of coverage of the 2015 Nepal earthquake, for example, The New Humanitarian was found to cover a wider range of topics and to focus on the voice of affected citizens more often, with few efforts to dramatise events – compared to Reuters. Similarly, our analysis of reporting of Yemen and South Sudan showed that Devex's coverage was very different from reporting by more mainstream news outlets, as it had a strong focus on economics and local/international businesses.

Despite their importance, the routines and practices operating within these specialist news outlets have not been studied before. Instead, previous research into international news coverage of humanitarian affairs has focused primarily on analysing the *content* of mainstream journalistic reporting, either in large international broadcasters (Franks 2006; Robertson 2015) or major national news outlets (Hawkins 2011; Yann and Bissell 2015; Ardèvol-Abreu 2016; Zerback and Holzleitner 2017). These kinds of analyses can do much: helping us to identify a list of likely factors that influence coverage. But they cannot tell us how these factors interact with one another in different contexts, how they change over time and how they are influenced by other less readily observable or predictable dynamics such as access, safety concerns and relations with sources. In other words, studies of media content shed little light on how processes of news production and selection are constantly negotiated through the actions of particular journalists in specific circumstances.

The few studies which have directly studied the professional practices underpinning international news coverage of humanitarian affairs have focused almost exclusively on mainstream journalism (see Imison and Chapman 2012; Cottle 2013; Cooper 2018; Kotišová 2019; Nolan, Brookes and Imison 2020; Lawson 2021). Indeed, Cooper (2018:237) concludes her study of social media's influence on news coverage of humanitarian disasters by arguing that the 'subset of journalists who manage to inhabit two different fields [of journalism and humanitarianism]... warrant more investigation'. The same focus on mainstream journalistic practices is also reflected in the significant body of research examining relations between humanitarian NGOs and journalists (Cottle and Nolan 2007; Powers 2018; Wright 2018). In this book, we aim to address this important gap by asking four key questions:

1   How do humanitarian journalists define their professional practices? (Chapter 2)

2   What news values and sourcing practices do humanitarian journalists adopt? (Chapter 3)
3   How do humanitarian journalists understand the concept of 'humanitarianism'? (Chapter 4)
4   How do humanitarian journalists relate to each other? (Chapter 5)

Book layout

In this book, we draw on the key principles of 'field theory' to help to explain how journalistic practice is shaped by a complex interaction of political, economic and social forces, alongside individual agency (Bourdieu 1998; Benson and Neveu 2005; Fligstein and McAdam 2012). However, almost all previous studies have used field theory to help explain what happens either inside, or outside professional fields like journalism and humanitarianism. In **Chapter 1,** we argue, instead, that the kinds of professional practiced adopted by humanitarian journalists are best explained by thinking about them as taking place within a 'thick boundary zone' (Eyal 2013) between the journalistic and humanitarian fields. Eyal (2013:168) suggests that all social fields, 'secrete these thick boundary zones as an inevitable aspect of their functioning, as fuzzy zones of separation and connection... characterised by qualities such as permeability, fuzziness, hybridity and weak institutionalization'. This general idea – and Eyal (2013) and Eyal and Pok's (2011) more specific concepts of boundary work, strategic ambiguity and a 'space of opportunity' – help us make sense of humanitarian journalists' practices, throughout our analysis.

According to Eyal (2013), the first step in understanding and explaining the professional norms and practices of actors at a 'boundary zone', is to establish how they position themselves in relation to different social fields: in this case, the fields of journalism and humanitarianism. In **Chapter 2**, we show that humanitarian journalists adopt the role of journalists but not 'mainstream' journalists, and humanitarian communicators but 'more objective' ones. We also reveal the implications this has for their funding, credibility, autonomy, role perceptions and especially their 'watchdog' function.

In **Chapter 3,** we investigate humanitarian journalists' news values and sourcing practices. We find that they take advantage of the relative freedom provided by their seemingly liminal status – at a boundary zone between fields – to experiment with other ways of performing the role of both a journalist and humanitarian. They rejected various mainstream journalistic practices – including the news values of 'cultural proximity' and 'immediacy' and the sourcing practices of 'humanisation' and a 'hierarchy of credibility' – in favour of hybrid practices that are neither entirely journalistic nor humanitarian but that, 'must be seen as native to the interface between the two' (Eyal and Pok 2011:16). These include 'reporting under-reported crises', 'adding value' to existing coverage and 'amplifying marginalised voices'.

In **Chapter 4**, we examine how the humanitarian journalists in our study understand the contested concept of 'humanitarianism' and how this shapes their practice. We find that they adopt an 'ambiguous humanitarianism', characterised by relatively broad and inconsistent understandings of the concept. We argue that maintaining such conceptual ambiguity is both an outcome of humanitarian journalist's field position and strategically valuable to them because it allows them more creative room to experiment with novel, hybrid practices. It also allows them to examine the political drivers of humanitarian crises in ways that conventional journalism often avoids.

In **Chapter 5,** we ask how humanitarian journalists relate to each other. We show that they are very weakly institutionalised because of a lack of competition, shared identity, field-building actors and, in many cases, even awareness of each other. We also document the differences between humanitarian journalists' norms and practices and those operating within news outlets that remain firmly within the journalistic field, such as Al Jazeera English and the Thomson Reuters Foundation. In the process, we show that there is not (yet) a unique field of 'humanitarian journalism' that supports and regulates humanitarian journalists' practices.

In the **concluding chapter**, we summarise the key features of humanitarian journalists' practice and argue that they provide an important complement to conventional news coverage. We emphasise that while humanitarian journalists may occupy a 'space of opportunity' it is also a space of marginalisation, precarity and potential co-option. However, we caution that support for humanitarian journalism must be mindful of a tension – that efforts to strengthen their professional standing may inadvertently undermine some of the defining aspects of their practice. Finally, we reflect on the wider implications of our analysis, including the blind spots within Eyal (2013) and Eyal and Pok's (2011) conceptual framework, the significance of non-institutionalised practices and what it really means to practice specialised forms of journalism.

Chapter notes

Table 0.1 Volume of online news coverage of the 40 largest humanitarian crises in 2021

Country	No. of News Articles
Afghanistan	475,744
Syria	230,000
Haiti	180,000
Lebanon	171,000
Yemen	121,000
Ethiopia	87,172
Iraq	62,926
Bangladesh	58,900
Turkey	57,000
Congo	50,200
Jordan	41,100
Palestine	38,700
Somalia	26,655
South Sudan	25,200
Venezuela	24,200
Nigeria	15,971
Uganda	15,000
Iran	14,200
Mali	13,827
Myanmar	13,500
Pakistan	13,100
Madagascar	9,190
Cameroon	8,290
Chad	8,288
Sudan	7,880
Democratic Republic of the Congo / DRC	6,456
Mozambique	5,790
Democratic People's Republic of Korea	5,570
Libya	5,010
Burkina Faso	4,844
El Salvador	4,380
Honduras	3,920
Zimbabwe	2,803
Niger	2,774
Burundi	2,265
Colombia	2,136
Guatemala	1,644
Central African Republic	1,459
Malawi	832
Ukraine	801
Zambia	512

Data provided by Care International and Meltwater.

Notes

1 More than 1.8 million online articles were analysed by the media monitoring service Meltwater between 1st January and 30th September 2021. Included were all countries where at least 1 million people were affected by conflict or climate-related disasters. The analysis is based on online articles in Arabic, English, French, German, and Spanish. This research was commissioned by Care International, who agreed to allow us to publish these results.

2 The sample period for the analysis of news coverage of each of these events was as follows: The conflict in South Sudan (September 2016 to December 2016) (n=7691); The 2016 Aceh earthquake (7 December 2016) (n=4279); The World Humanitarian Summit (23 May 2016 to 24 May 2016) (n=745) and The 2017 UN appeal for humanitarian funding (4 December 2016) (n=334).

3 Humanosphere subsequently closed in 2017 due to a loss of funding.

4 In January 2018, we carried out a survey of individuals who were either directly or indirectly involved in the aid or development sector, in partnership with The New Humanitarian/IRIN. This survey included both The New Humanitarian's readers and non-readers. A section of the survey focused specifically on perceptions of The New Humanitarian's coverage, but respondents were also asked about their media preferences and habits in general. In total, 1,626 respondents completed the survey, including individuals working for International NGOs (28%), the United Nations (9%), academia (9%), national or local NGOs (8%), government organisations (8%) and in the corporate sector (5%). A majority of respondents were either mid-career (32%) or senior professionals (41%) and had either 'some' (34%) or a 'significant' amount (30%) of decision-making authority within their organisation. For more details of the method and findings from this study, see 'Attitudes towards humanitarian news within the aid sector' (Scott, Wright and Bunce 2018b).

5 This analysis involved a combination of content analysis and framing analysis. The sample period consisted of all news items produced by Reuters (including the Thomson Reuters Foundation) and IRIN News within the first 13 days after the Nepal earthquake (25.4.15 – 7.5.15). We included all conventional news reports and special reports/features, and photo features that had accompanying commentary. In total, 27 articles from Reuters and 17 from IRIN News qualified for inclusion in the study. In each article, we analyse which sources were quoted, the topic focus and the framing of the disaster. For more details of the method and findings from this study, see 'The State of Humanitarian Journalism' (Scott, Wright and Bunce 2018a).

6 These news organisations were chosen because they represent both some of the most prolific international producers of humanitarian news and a diversity of forms of funding, focus and format. To identify relevant content, the website of each news outlet was searched using keywords related to the conflicts. Only original articles referring directly to the conflicts in South Sudan and Yemen and the humanitarian consequences were included in the analysis. The sample period for news about South Sudan was the six months from 18th February 2017, while for Yemen it was the six months from 15th April 2017. For more details of the method and findings from this study, see 'The State of Humanitarian Journalism' (Scott, Wright and Bunce 2018a).

References

Adams, W. (1986). Whose Lives Count?: TV Coverage of Natural Disasters. *Journal of Communication*. 36. 113–122.

Alexander, J. (2022). Aid Policy Trends to Watch in 2022. The New Humanitarian. Published and accessed on 3 January 2022. https://www.thenewhumanitarian.org/analysis/2022/1/3/aid-policy-trends-to-watch-in-2022

Alexander, J. and Rozzell, J. (2022). Is Ukraine's Aid Bonanza Coming at the Expense of Other Crises? The New Humanitarian. First published and accessed on 24 March 2022. https://www.thenewhumanitarian.org/analysis/2022/03/24/ukraine-aid-funding-media-other-crises

Ardèvol-Abreu, A. (2016). The Framing of Humanitarian Crises in the Spanish Media: An Inductive Approach. *Revista Española de Investigaciones Sociológicas*. 155. 37–54.

Bacon, W. and Nash, C. (2004). Stories in Distress: Three Case Studies in Australian Media Coverage of Humanitarian Crises. *Australian Journalism Review*. 26:1. 19–39.

Barnett, M. (2011). *Empire of Humanity: A History of Humanitarianism*. Cornell University Press.

Benson, R. and Neveu, E. (2005). *Bourdieu and the Journalistic Field*. Polity Press.

Bourdieu, P. (1993). The Field of Cultural Production. Essays on Art and Literature. In Johnson, R. (Ed.), Polity Press.

Bourdieu, P. (1998). *On Television*. New Press [trans. P. Parkhurst Ferguson].

Brommesson, D. and Ekengren, A. M. (2017). *The Mediatization of Foreign Policy: Political Decision Making and Humanitarian Intervention*. Palgrave MacMillan.

Brown, P. H. and Minty, J. (2006). *Media Coverage and Charitable Giving after the 2004 Tsunami*. William Davidson Institute Working Paper No. 855.

Care International. (2021). *Suffering in Silence: The 10 Most Under-Reported Humanitarian Crises of 2020*. Care International.

Care International. (2022). *Suffering in Silence: The 10 Most Under-Reported Humanitarian Crises of 2021*. Care International.

Chouliaraki, L. (2006). *The Spectatorship of Suffering*. Sage Publications.

Cohen, S. (2001). *States of Denial: Knowing about Atrocities and Suffering*. Polity and Blackwell Publishers.

Cohen, M. S., Riffe, D. and Kim, S. (2021). Media and Money: A 50 Year Analysis of International News Coverage and US Foreign Aid. *The Journal of International Communication*. 27:2. 172–191.

Cooper, G. (2018). Reporting Humanitarian Disasters in a Social Media Age. Routledge.

Cooper, G. (2020). #AidToo: Social Media Spaces and the Transformation of the Reporting of Aid Scandals in 2018. *Journalism Practice*. 15:6. 747–766.

Cottle, S. (2013). Journalists Witnessing Disaster: From the Calculus of Death to the Injunction to Care. *Journalism Studies*. 14:2. 232–248.

Cottle, S. and Cooper, G. (Eds.). (2019). *Humanitarianism, Communications and Change*. Peter Lang.

Cottle, S. and Nolan, D. (2007). Global Humanitarianism and the Changing Aid-Media Field. *Journalism Studies*. 8:6. 862–878.

Davies, L. (2022). Hunger Crisis Grips Horn of Africa – But 80% of Britons Unaware, Poll Shows. The Guardian. First published and accessed on 12 May 2022. https://www.theguardian.com/global-development/2022/may/12/hunger-crisis-drought-grips-horn-of-africa-but-80-of-britons-unaware-poll-shows

Deuze, M. and Witschge, T. (2017). Beyond Journalism: Theorizing the Transformation of Journalism. *Journalism*. 19:2. 165–181.

Eyal, G. (2013). Spaces between Fields. In Gorski, P. (Ed.), Bourdieu and Historical Analysis. Duke University Press. 158–182.

Eyal, G. and Pok, G. (2011). From a Sociology of Professions to a Sociology of Expertise. *Expert Determination Electronic Law Journal*. https://www.semanticscholar.org/paper/From-a-sociology-of-professions-to-a-sociology-of-Eyal-Pok/e0fba82e8e40aba82e8ea0e771b3d228d0ce30c4#citing-papers

Ferron, B., Kotišová, J. and Smith, S. (2022). The Primacy of Secondary Things: A Sustained Scientific Dialogue on Three Edges of the Journalistic Field. *Journal Media*. 3. 212–227.

Fligstein, N. and McAdam, M. (2012). *A Theory of Fields*. Oxford University Press.

Franks, S. (2006). The CARMA Report on Western Media Coverage of Humanitarian Disasters. *The Political Quarterly*. 77:2. 281–284.

FTS. (2021). *Appeals and Response Plans*. OCHA Financial Tracking Service (FTS).

Gutiérrez, J. and García, R. (2011). Assessing the Humanitarian Framing of the Spanish Press Coverage of the Darfur Crisis. *Ecquid Novi: African Journalism Studies*. 32:1. 66–81.

Hall, S., Critcher, C., Jefferson, T., et al. (1978). *Policing the Crisis: Mugging, the State, and Law and Order*. Macmillan.

Hawkins, V. (2011). Media Selectivity and the Other Side of the CNN Effect: The Consequences of Not Paying Attention to Conflict. *Media, War and Conflict*. 4:1. 55–68.

Hopgood, S. (2008). Saying "No" to Wal-Mart? In Fassin, D. and Pandolfi, M. (Eds.), *States of Emergency*. Zone Books. 98–123.

Imison, M. and Chapman, S. (2012). Australian Journalists' Reflections on Local Coverage of a Health-Related Story from the Developing World. *Australian Journalism Review*. 34:1. 93–107.

IPCC. (2022). Climate Change: A Threat to Human Wellbeing and Health of the Planet. Taking Action Now Can Secure Our Future. United Nations Intergovernmental Panel on Climate Change. Published and accessed on 28 February 2022. https://www.ipcc.ch/2022/02/28/pr-wgii-ar6/

Joye, S. (2009). The Hierarchy of Global Suffering. *The Journal of International Communication*. 15:2. 45–61.

Kotišová, J. (2019). *Crisis Reporters, Emotions, and Technology: An Ethnography.* Springer.

Krause, M. (2014). *The Good Project: Humanitarian Relief NGOs and the Fragmentation of Reason.* University of Chicago Press.

Kwak, H. and An, J. (2014). *Understanding News Geography and Major Determinants of Global News Coverage of Disasters.* Computation and Journalism Symposium '14, New York.

Laichter, J. (2021). Frontline Lives: The Ukrainian Children Growing Up with War. The New Humanitarian. First published and accessed on 18 October 2021. Available online at https://www.thenewhumanitarian.org/photo-feature/2021/10/18/Europe-frontline-lives-Ukrainian-children-growing-up-with-war

Lawson, B. T. (2021). Hiding Behind Databases, Institutions and Actors: How Journalists Use Statistics in Reporting Humanitarian Crises. *Journalism Practice.* https://www.tandfonline.com/doi/citedby/10.1080/17512786.2021.1930106?scroll=top&needAccess=true

Medvetz, T. (2012). *Think Tanks in America.* University of Chicago Press.

Nolan, D., Brookes, S. and Imison, M. (2020). Abandoning Either/Ors in Analyzing Shifts in Humanitarian Reporting. *Journalism Practice.* 14:1. 17–33.

OCHA. (2022). *Global Humanitarian Overview 2022.* United Nations Office for the Coordination of Humanitarian Affairs.

Orgad, S. (2013). Visualizers of Solidarity: Organizational Politics in Humanitarian and International Development NGOs. *Visual Communication.* 12:3. 295–314.

Palmer, M. (2019). *International News Agencies: A History.* Springer.

Powers, M. (2018). *NGOs as Newsmakers.* Columbia University Press.

Powers, M. and Vera-Zambrano, S. (2023). *The Journalist's Predicament: A French-American Investigation.* Columbia University Press.

Robertson, A. (2015). *Global News: Reporting Conflicts and Cosmopolitanism.* Peter Lang.

Scott, M. (2018). Distant Suffering Online: The Unfortunate Irony of Cyber-Utopian Narratives. *International Communication Gazette.* 77:7. 637–653.

Scott, M., Wright, K. and Bunce, M. (2018a). *The State of Humanitarian Journalism.* University of East Anglia.

Scott, M., Wright, K. and Bunce, M. (2018b). *Attitudes Towards Humanitarian News within the Aid Sector.* University of East Anglia. City, University of London.

Scott, M., Bunce, M. and Wright, K. (2022). The Politics of Humanitarian Journalism. In Chouliaraki, L. and Vestergaard, A. (Eds.), *Routledge Handbook of Humanitarian Communication.* Routledge. 203–220.

Seu, I. B. and Orgad, S. (2017). *Caring in Crisis? Humanitarianism, the Public and NGOs.* Palgrave.

Sopova, A. and Taylor-Lind, A. (2021). Ukraine's Seven-Year War, and How COVID-19 Made Division Permanent. The New Humanitarian. First published and accessed on 6 April 2021. Available online at

https://www.thenewhumanitarian.org/feature/2021/4/5/Ukraine-war-
COVID-19-division-permanent

Stupart, R. (2020). Bearing Witness: Practices of Journalistic Witnessing in South Sudan. PhD thesis, LSE.

Stupart, R. (2021a). Tired, Hungry, and on Deadline: Affect and Emotion in the Practice of Conflict Journalism. *Journalism Studies*, 22:12. 1574–1589.

Stupart, R. (2021b). Feeling Responsible: Emotion and Practical Ethics in Conflict Journalism. *Media, War and Conflict*. 14:3. 268–281.

Stupart, R. (2022). Forgotten Conflicts: Journalists and the Humanitarian Imaginary. In Chouliaraki, L. and Vestergaard, A. (Eds.), *The Routledge Handbook of Humanitarian Communication*. Routledge.

van Belle, D., Rioux, J.-S. and Potter, D. (2004). *Media, Bureaucracies and Foreign Aid*. Palgrave MacMillan.

VSO. (2001). *The Live Aid Legacy: The Developing World Through British Eyes – A Research Report*. Voluntary Service Overseas.

Wright, K. (2018). *Who's Reporting Africa Now? Non-Governmental Organizations, Journalists and Multimedia*. Peter Lang.

Yan, Y. and Bissell, K. (2015). The Sky Is Falling: Predictors of News Coverage of Natural Disasters Worldwide. *Communication Research*. 45:6. 1–25.

Zerback, T. and Holzleitner, J. (2017). Under-Cover: The Influence of Event- and Context-Traits on the Visibility of Armed Conflicts in German Newspaper Coverage (1992–2013). *Journalism*. 19:3. 366–383.

1 Making news in a boundary zone

Our aim in this book is to understand the professional norms and practices used by humanitarian journalists and the factors that influence their reporting. When addressing such questions about the complex interaction of factors that shape news production, journalism studies frequently turns to 'field theory' (Bourdieu 1998; Fligstein and McAdam 2012; Maares and Hanusch 2020) – and for good reason. The concept of a 'field' provides a means of simultaneously considering the external and internal forces that shape professional practice. This is particularly welcome in journalism studies, where researchers have struggled to bridge the divide between macro-societal level approaches and micro-organisational approaches (Benson and Neveu 2005). Furthermore, the concepts of *doxa*, *capital* and *habitus* within field theory have been shown to provide versatile 'thinking tools' (Wacquant 1989:50) for taking account of key influences such as competition between news outlets and individual agency. We begin this chapter, therefore, by providing a brief introduction to these key concepts and by looking at how they have helped us to better understand specialist, transnational and corrective forms of news production, which share similarities with humanitarian journalists' practices.

However, we also argue that field theory has a blind spot when it comes to thinking about the norms and practices of peripheral actors who operate at the boundaries or intersection of multiple fields – as humanitarian journalists appear to. As Stampnitzky (2013:12) puts it, 'sites of action that cross multiple institutional fields, or that operate on the boundaries of fields, are apt to appear puzzling or hard to understand within this framework'. Therefore, following the work of Eyal (2013) and Eyal and Pok (2011), we suggest that it is useful to think of social fields, not as strictly bounded spaces, but as 'secret[ing]… thick boundary zones as an inevitable aspect of their functioning, as fuzzy zones of separation and connection' (Eyal 2013:174).

DOI: 10.4324/9781003356806-2

We also review previous research into other professional practices that appear to be located at a 'boundary zone', to help us to better understand the mechanisms which shape professional practice there. Such practices include those associated with think tanks (Medvetz 2012), terrorism studies (Stampnitzky 2013), pole studios (Fennell 2018) and hybrid wellness practices, such as alternative medicine and spiritual guidance (Lee 2004). Key features of professional practice within these social spaces include boundary work, creativity, hybridity and strategic ambiguity as well as an absence of symbolic differentiation, field-specific capital and field-building activities. We conclude that these concepts not only provide a useful framework for guiding our analysis of humanitarian journalists but may also offer a useful addition to journalism studies and field theory, by helping us analyse forms of expertise that are not fully institutionalised.

Journalism and humanitarianism as social fields

A field refers to a semi-autonomous sphere of action within society (Bourdieu 1998). Such spheres of social practice include the fields of sport, science, law, literature, art, politics, religion – and in our case – journalism and humanitarianism. While each of these fields is a 'microcosm, which has its own rules' and ways of doing things (Bourdieu 1998:44), they are also shaped by wider political and economic forces in society and by their relationship with other social fields.

The autonomy of a field – or how free it is to determine its own norms and practices – varies according to how dominated it is by the wider 'field of power', or social system. This is because forces and logics found in the 'wider field' may enter into and 'colonise' the internal logic of sub-fields. Researchers have explored, for example, how market forces have come to dominate the journalistic logic, although the nature and extent of this domination varies between countries (Bourdieu 1998; Champagne 2005).

Internally, fields are structured around those organisations that are 'purest' and most independent of state power, political power and economic power and therefore most guided and committed to the values of their specific professional field. Within the journalistic field, this includes news outlets such as the BBC, while in the humanitarian field, this includes organisations such as the International Committee of the Red Cross (ICRC) and Médecins Sans Frontières (MSF) – as shown in Figure 1.1. At the periphery of the field, are those organisations that are most dependent on external powers and commercial interests (Bourdieu 2005:41) – factors that are sometimes described as 'pollution' because they may prevent organisations from following the core values of their professional field. So, for example, the main 'pollution' that poses threats to the 'purity' of the humanitarian field have been shown to be donor governments, social movements and religious organisations (Krause 2014:113), as is illustrated in Figure 1.1. In her book, *The Good Project*, Krause details how the position of humanitarian organisations in this field impacts the work they do – as well as the authority and influence they wield over others.

Within a field, people and institutions are positioned relative to each other according to their influence, or capital. Bourdieu (1984) describes the capital, which agents compete for, as not only financial but also symbolic. Examples of symbolic capital within the journalistic field include the prestige or status associated with winning or being nominated for a journalistic prize, or holding a national office in a national press organisation. Bourdieu (1984) argues that actors use this

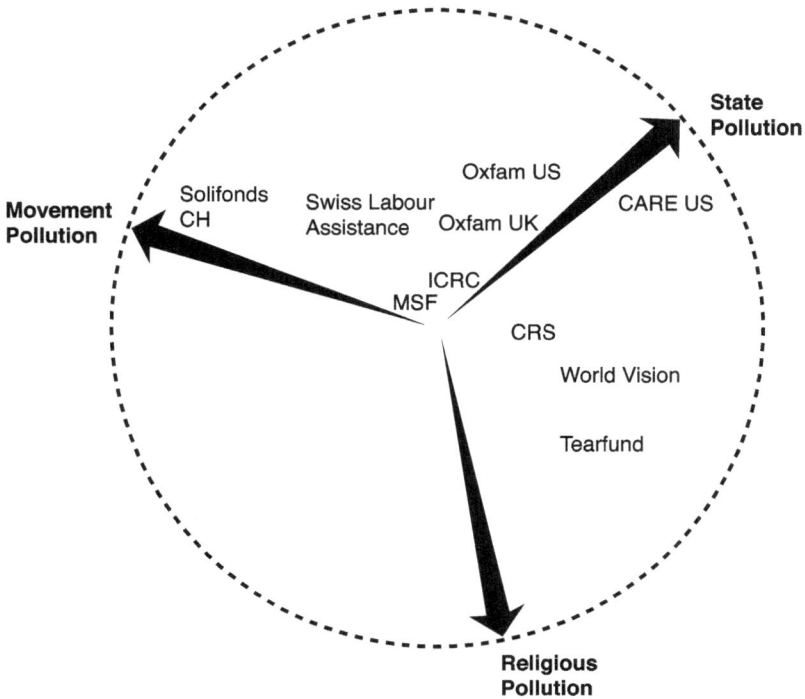

Figure 1.1 Purity and pollution in the humanitarian field.

Source: Used with permission of Monika Krause, from The Good Project (Krause 2014). Permission conveyed through Copyright Clearance Center.

field-specific, symbolic capital to differentiate amongst themselves, to establish their relative position within the field.

However, more recent theoretical work (Örnebring et al. 2018) has revised Bourdieu's model: arguing convincingly that 'financial capital' should be split into two, analytically distinct categories. The first relates to a journalist's *access to material resources*: that is, the 'economic, managerial, collegial and technological resources available to individual journalists in the immediate context in which they perform their work' (Örnebring et al. 2018:410). The second involves a journalist's *personal material security*: that is, the 'degree of contractual and financial security' possessed by the journalist. As the authors argue, 'high-level access to resources often correlate with a high degree of material security, but this is not always the case' (Örnebring et al. 2018:409).

Every social field also has its own shared, internal logic or 'rules of the game'. Bourdieu (1993) calls these doxa, or 'a universe of tacit presuppositions' that help to organise action within the field. Important doxic values within the journalistic field, for example, include the general notion of 'newsworthiness' – that is, the idea that one event can be more 'newsworthy' than another in an objective sense – as well as doxic beliefs about the importance of objectivity, autonomy, public service, neutrality and timeliness (Markham 2011). However, adherence to these doxic values pre-supposes that actors within a field agree that the struggle for recognition and dominance is 'worth it'. This belief that the 'game' of competing for capital within a given field is 'worth playing' – which helps to sustain a field – is referred to as '*illusio*' (Bourdieu 1993).

In the humanitarian field, dominant doxic values include independence, and moral equivalence: that is, the notion that the suffering of any human being is equally worthy of attention, care and relief, regardless of nationality or any other affiliation (Barnett 2011). However, the orientation of humanitarianism to politics is highly contested, and this contestation is used by actors to differentiate themselves from competitors. Within the Europe and the USA, professional humanitarian agencies have been shaped by the 'chemical' branch of humanitarianism, which focuses on politically neutral forms of emergency relief (Barnett 2011). But there are struggles within and between humanitarian agencies that are shaped by tensions between these values and those of the 'alchemical' branch of humanitarianism, which aims to expose and challenge the structural causes of suffering (Barnett 2011). The tension between these two strands of thought was highly visible at the World Humanitarian Summit in 2015. There, friction emerged between actors in favour of aligning humanitarian action more closely with conflict-resolution and the UN's Sustainable Development Goals (Aneja 2016), and more traditional organisations, such as the ICRC, which expressed concern that politicising humanitarian aid undermined important humanitarian principles, as well as harming aid agencies' ability to intervene between combatants (Maurer 2014).

Even non-traditional donors, which are not members of the intergovernmental Development Assistance Committee (DAC), are subject to the dominant doxic values of the humanitarian field, although they may use their contestation of some of these values to differentiate themselves from their Western counterparts. For example, China pursues a South-to-South and state-to-state approach to 'humanitarian diplomacy', which openly privileges its neighbours in the Asia-Pacific region, as well as trade and strategic partners, particularly in sub-Saharan Africa (Krebs 2016; Gong 2021). In this way, China critiques what it sees as the imperialistic approaches of American and European governments, and Western non-governmental organisations. Nevertheless, other non-traditional donors are increasingly signalling their acceptance of some or all of the dominant doxic values of the field. For example, Saudi Arabia previously gave aid through a multiplicity of religious foundations and charities, in ways which were shaped by politicised ideas of Islamic solidarity, and the need to provide for the Muslim *ummah* (Derbal 2022). However, KSRelief – which is the most centralised mechanism for delivering aid, associated with the Saudi royal family – increasingly stresses the value of moral equivalence, albeit in ways which are still shaped by ideas about Muslim charitable obligations, such as *zakat* and *da'awa* (Al Yahya and Fustier 2011; Moussa 2014; Derbal 2022).

Nevertheless, some of the most dominant doxic values of the humanitarian field are not abstract norms, but are embedded in humanitarian practice itself. These include conceptualisations of 'adding value', or the principle of 'making the most difference' (Krause 2014:31). According to Krause (2014), desk officers and directors of operations in humanitarian INGOs frequently emphasise the importance of 'adding value' when explaining why they start a new project. The key factors they consider include; limitations on resources, logistical challenges, the capacity and expertise of the agency itself and their relationship to what other agencies are doing. Given these issues, Krause (2014:31–36) argues that international relief agencies decide where to go and who to help, based, not only on the principle of providing 'relief to those who need it most', but also on a consideration of where they can 'add the most value'. As one desk officer put it, 'first of all we need to think about whether we really have the skills and capacity to make a difference' (Krause 2014:31).

A final key concept within field theory's 'analytical tool box' is 'habitus'. This refers to the set of dispositions, formed over an agent's lifetime of experience and socialisation, which shape their perceptions and practice. As Swartz (1998:101) puts it, 'habitus evokes the idea of a set of deeply internalized master dispositions that generate action'. But while agents are influenced by the values and expectations of their habitus, they also have their own agency – thinking and acting in their own unique and often strategic ways, in response to their current circumstances (Webb et al. 2002:58). Given this, the concept of habitus links agency and structure, by describing 'a structuring structure, which organises practices and perception of practices' (Bourdieu and Wacquant 1992).

An agent's habitus is also dynamic and may change and grow as they absorb and develop a professional habitus, within a field. Journalists, for example, are sometimes said to have an early habitus (shaped by parents, childhood, school education), as well as a second, journalistic habitus (Bourdieu 1984:171). Schultz (2007:193) refers to this as journalists' "professional habitus", a mastering of a specific, professional game in a specific professional field'. Thus, in journalism, says Neveu (2007:339), it is common for a process of 'habitus transformation' to occur when a journalist enters the field – either for the first time, or when they change roles. Markham notes (2011) that new foreign correspondents may have higher levels of enthusiasm and a greater concern with ethical values, partly because they are fresh out of journalism school, but that this falls over time, with journalists often becoming more cynical over the course of their professional trajectory.

Global, corrective and specialised forms of journalism

Field theory – and the concepts of capital, habitus and doxa – has been widely embraced within media studies to help understand journalistic production (e.g., Champagne 1993; Hovden 2001; Couldry 2003; Duval 2005; Hallin 2005; Marchetti 2005; Schudson 2005; Hesmondhaulgh 2006; Neveu 2007; Dickenson 2008; Mellor 2008;). Within these studies of the journalistic field, three strands of research are particularly relevant to our study of humanitarian journalists.

First, field theory has been used to help understand the professional values and practices within news outlets that operate transnationally, producing content for audiences around the world, just as the journalists and news outlets in our study do. Biesla (2008) argues that such transnational news outlets occupy a *global* field of journalism, and that this was initially established through the competitive struggles between international news agencies such as AFP, AP and Reuters. As they competed with one another to expand their networks, particularly after the end of World War II, these newswires adopted a globalist approach to newsgathering characterised by a degree of freedom from territorial allegiance to any one specific country. Horvit (2006), for example, analyses the newswire coverage of the Iraq War and finds that, in their reporting, the wires did not privilege sources from their 'home' countries: AFP did not quote more French officials; Reuters did not quote more British officials; and AP did not quote more US officials. Moreover, in analysing the tone and direction of coverage, Horvit (2006) finds the newswires' story content did not reflect the political position of their home countries towards the military action.

However, these newswires are not completely independent of national or regional influences. Although they are global in reach, and broadly free from specific national affiliations, the international news agencies are still characterised by the journalistic norms and values of the West: a function of their competitive position in the global journalistic field. Furthermore, given their declining revenues, these newswires are locked in fierce competition to be first with the news. Williams (2011:78) notes that, in this context, 'rather than a set of news criteria, the values of news should be seen in terms of what clients and subscribers are willing to pay for. Giving customers what they want is crucial'. One of the most significant implications of this customer-orientated approach has been, Williams (2011) and others suggests, a focus on news that is Western-centric: customers are based in the Global North, they pay for the news, and it is to them that the newswires cater. The focus on Western customers – and the fact that newswires export their news to the Global South, homogenising and skewing global discourse in this direction (Biesla 2008) – has long been a source of controversy. It sparked UNESCO's New World Information and Communications Order (NWICO) debates of the 1970s (McBride 1980), and it continues to concern commentators today. In addition, analyses of CNN's output have shown that it tends to be uncritically supportive of U.S. foreign policy (Thussu 2000). Other forms of commercially funded transnational journalism practiced in Belgium, France and the United Kingdom have also been found to be shaped by the staff, cultural perspectives and political interests of news organisations (Denĉik 2013; Christin 2016; Van Leuven and Berglez 2016).

Second, field theory has been used to understand the norms and practices of journalists and news outlets that claim to adhere to more ethical alternative practices, compared with the dominant doxic norms and values reproduced by 'incumbents' within the journalistic field. Common forms of such 'ethically corrective journalism' (Berglez 2013) include solutions journalism (McIntyre 2019; McIntyre and Lough 2021), peace journalism (Galtung 2003; Lynch and McGoldrick 2005), development journalism (Domatob and Hall 1983; Xiaoge 2009), conflict-sensitive reporting (Shaw and Selvarajah 2019), global journalism (Berglez 2013) and counter-hegemonic journalism (Painter 2008). One of the most successful examples of counter-hegemonic journalism is Al Jazeera English. It seeks to tell the news from a Middle Eastern perspective and challenge the dominance of Western news values (Miles 2005; Figenschou 2011; Ghanem 2021). In doing so, it often 'portrays a concealed reality: it displays the images of war and death that no American television network will show; it gives airtime to the people who will be barred from appearing in any other network' (Biesla 2008:362).

Despite this, Al Jazeera English is still very firmly within the journalistic field. It remains engaged in a strategic game within the global field whose basic rules were determined long before its entry. Al Jazeera English looks to the other major players in the field as its competition (and inspiration); it similarly provides news packaged to fulfil the needs of its audience; and it operates by the norms of the global journalistic field. For example, it does not generally challenge the basic doxic value of objectivity that pervades and informs the global journalistic field. The channel was set up,

> explicitly embracing the media values of objectivity, accuracy and balanced, factual reporting, and modelling itself after the Western media tradition of the BBC (where many of its staff were trained) and CNN (the channel it seeks to imitate and compete with).
>
> (Biesla 2008:362–363)

As Miles (2005:412) notes, Al Jazeera English was launched with the purpose of 'communicating with the West in its own language'. Indeed, Bielsa (2008) argues that the narrative forms and values of Western journalism are today so pervasive, that their adoption is a precondition for successful participation in global news markets, as is evident even in the case of Al-Jazeera English. The same is true for all other forms of corrective journalism. While they may adjust some of their professional practices to offer an alternative perspective they still operate very much within the journalistic field because that is how they establish their credibility and influence.

Third, field theory has been used to understand the production practices of journalists and news outlets reporting on specific subject areas, or news 'beats', such as sport (English 2015), economics (Duval 2005) or international affairs (Carroll 2006). Marchetti (2005) argues that, within the journalistic field, there is an opposition between a 'generalist' pole and a 'specialized' pole. While the later may, in general, have relatively less autonomy, this varies significantly between different types of media outlet and there are also significant differences between different subfields (see Tunstall 1971). These differences are determined by, amongst other things, their internal position within the professional hierarchy and their proximity to either the intellectual or commercial pole (Marchetti 2005). For example, as illustrated in Figure 1.2, international journalism's proximity to the intellectual, rather than the commercial pole means that is generally associated with greater journalistic, rather than economic capital (Carroll 2006; English 2015). Put another way, reporting of international affairs is associated with professional prestige, but it rarely directly generates significant advertising and audience revenue. Furthermore, international journalism generates less capital overall than most other news beats – as is illustrated by its position relative on the y-axis in Figure 1.2. This helps to explain why coverage of foreign affairs is often amongst the first to be cut, in response to the growing financial pressures faced by most news outlets (Sambrook 2010).

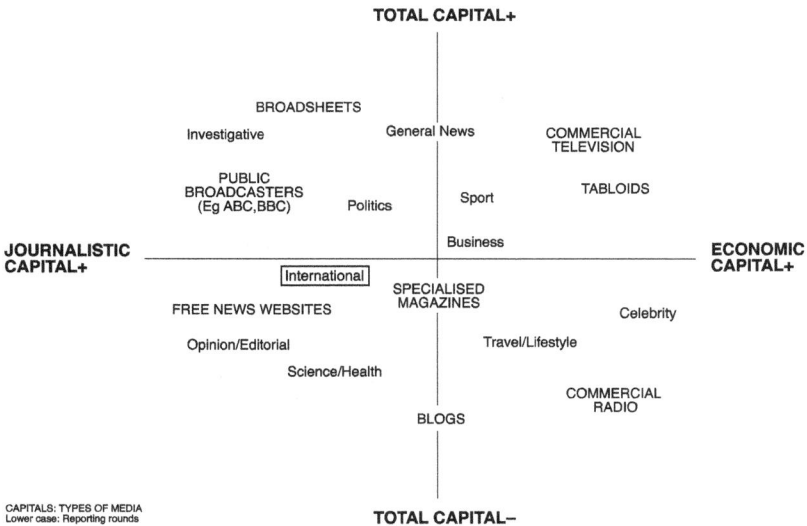

Figure 1.2 International journalism in the journalistic field.

Source: Adapted with permission of Peter English, from 'Mapping the sports journalism field' (English 2015:1005). Permission conveyed through Copyright Clearance Center.

Marchetti (2005) also identifies several variables that help to explain the relationship between specialised subfields of journalism and the social spaces they report on. These include the degree of interrelation between their respective economies, the degree of political control of their activities and the degree to which one imposes its problematic and principals of hierarchisation on the other. For example, Powers (2015:187) argues that INGOs – like Amnesty International, Human Rights Watch and Oxfam – are 'expanding the boundaries of journalism' by increasingly taking on a number of seemingly journalistic functions, such as providing timing, credibly and diverse information from abroad. Despite this, Powers (2015) also argues that the norms and practices of the journalistic field continue to shape the sorts of 'news' that INGOs produce because this is what is valued by the political elites, which INGOs are seeking to appeal to.

In summary, these three strands of research each help us to understand particular aspects of the transnational, corrective and specialised practices of the humanitarian journalists in our study. They suggest that humanitarian journalists should be understood as competing globally, as well as nationally, that they may define their practices at least partially in opposition to conventional journalistic norms, that they are likely to generate less capital than most other news beats, and that they are more likely to generate symbolic, rather than economic capital. However, we have also shown that existing research in these areas remains rooted to a particular view of the journalistic field. They assume – as do almost all applications of field theory – that professional practices fall neatly either inside or outside of a social field. As Eyal (2013:158) puts it, they maintain a view of fields as, 'distinct spheres whose contents are clearly bounded and well distinguished from one another'. For example, although transnational news outlets may not be (heavily) constrained by national fields, they are still understood to operate within a *global* journalistic field. Similarly, while those practicing corrective forms of journalism may present themselves as offering alternatives to conventional doxic practices, they are still understood as sitting firmly within the journalistic field, albeit in a non-central position. Finally, when studying the interaction of specialised journalistic sub-fields with the fields they are covering, the concern is with whether their respective boundaries 'expand or contract' (Powers 2015:187) and the extent to which the doxa of one field gets adopted by another. As Powers (2015:198) argues, while NGOs may be increasingly acting as journalistic entities, 'the boundaries between journalists and NGOs are well understood by all involved… NGOs understand that what they do is different from journalism'.

Even those studies which have focused specifically on examining what happens at the periphery of the journalistic field have often maintained a view of fields as having relatively distinct 'edges' (Ferron, Kotišová and Smith 2022). For example, Eldridge (2018) has examined how a range of new, online media actors – including Gawker, reddit, Breitbart and WikiLeaks – have 'challenged us to think differently about the journalistic field'. However, his central argument is simply that these 'interloper media' have 'broadened' ideas of what constitutes journalism. Similarly, Schapals (2022:12) concludes from his study of seemingly peripheral or quasi-journalistic actors that, 'despite their deviant traits, they offer something that is functionally equivalent to journalism'. But what if it were possible to do more than just broaden, contract or strengthen the journalistic field boundary (Carlson and Lewis 2015)? What if actors were able to inhabit the social space occupied by the boundary itself? How would that shape their relationship with different fields, their respective capital and doxa, and what implications would this have for their professional norms and practices?

Wright (2016, 2018) began to address these questions when she argued that complex moral economies span the boundaries between the journalistic and humanitarian fields, which are constructed through the constant interaction of the economic and normative values involved in both fields. Her research focuses on particular kinds of exchange systems: journalists' use (and legitimation) of multimedia produced or commissioned by aid agencies, which is often dependent upon, and enacted through, freelancers who move back and forth between journalistic and humanitarian organisations (Wright 2016). In this way, she concludes, they blur the boundary between humanitarianism and journalism, whilst also reconstructing it via normative ideas about freelancers' autonomy and intermediary organisations, such as photographic agencies (Wright 2016). Thus Wright (2015) concludes that there is a need to pay more analytical attention to 'these grey areas' which exist at the boundaries between fields. But what if there are other actors, practices and political economies worth attending to in the 'grey areas' between the humanitarian and journalistic fields? This is the question we address in the next section.

Working at a 'boundary zone'

The idea that field boundaries have their own volume, which actors can occupy, has been articulated in most detail by Eyal (2006, 2013) and Eyal and Pok (2011). They suggest that we think of the boundary as a thick zone of interface and overlap (Eyal 2006), or trading zone that both separates and connects fields (Eyal 2013). In full, Eyal (2013:63) proposed that,

> We cease to think of the boundary... as a fine line with no width to it, and begin to grasp it as a real social entity with its own volume, so to speak. As such, the boundary does not simply separate what's inside and outside the field, e.g. what is economic and what is not, but is also a zone of essential connections and transactions between them.

Eyal (2013) points out that the idea of a 'boundary zone' was also briefly suggested by Bourdieu (1996) in his analysis of the Salons of mid-19th century French High Society Ladies. Bourdieu (1996:51–53) characterised these salons as 'bastard institutions' that served as 'genuine articulations between the political and artistic fields' because they enabled writers and politicians to interact in ways that that were not possible elsewhere. While some politicians could acquire influence that was not possible in the political sphere, writers could act as a pressure group for material or symbolic rewards (Eyal 2013).

Unfortunately, very little empirical research has employed the idea of a 'boundary zone'. In one of the few exceptions, Stampnitzky's (2013:7) study of terrorism expertise demonstrates that this profession has not 'been fully 'disciplined''. She argues that, despite becoming the dominant framework for understanding illegitimate political violence, the concept of 'terrorism' remains unstable, determined by constant conflicts over its meaning. Expert discourse on 'terrorism' should, therefore, be understood as, 'operating at the contested boundary between politics and science, between academic expertise and the state... [in] a space that straddles several "fields"' (Stampnitzky 2013). She concludes by observing that,

> The case of terrorism expertise may, in fact, be only one of many examples of the organized production of expertise in liminal spaces, a set of cases that have largely been neglected in favor of a focus on more strictly institutionalized sites of knowledge production.
>
> (Stampnitzky 2011:7)

Similarly, Fennell (2018) argues that the diverse and ambiguous practices within pole studios in the US offer another empirical case of a set of practices at the intersection of multiple fields. Specifically, since poling can be interpreted as an erotic dance, a fitness activity, an art form and a competitive sport, pole studios should be understood as creating and managing a social space at the boundary between the fields of the adult entertainment, art, fitness and sport. This emerging literature suggests three key concepts that help to explain practices that take place within the 'boundary zone'. These are: boundary work; spaces of opportunity; and strategic ambiguity.

Boundary work

'Boundary work' is central to understanding practices that take place in a boundary zone (Eyal 2013). Gieryn (1983) defines boundary work, with respect to the field of science, as the (rhetorical) methods through which scientists legitimate and differentiate themselves and their work from non-scientists. In the case of journalism, Carlson and Lewis (2015:14) describes boundary work as the performative struggles over the label of 'journalism', most commonly used to demarcate journalism from non-journalism. Such methods of demarcation include dismissing certain practices as 'not journalism' or defending journalistic autonomy from actors seeking to influence journalism.

However, Eyal (2013:164) argues that such conventional accounts of boundary work fail to ask, 'where is boundary work itself located? Inside the field or outside it? When scientists write op-ed pieces in order to expose charlatans, is this scientific or journalistic activity?'. Instead, such acts of distinction must be understood to take place at the site of the boundary itself. As Eyal (2013:174) puts it,

> While... the practices, symbolic materials and persons who serve as boundary signs... mark the boundary between two sides, they themselves belong to neither side. They are hybrid. Put differently, the very act of drawing boundaries by the same token also transgresses them. All of this serves merely to point out that, cartographically, it does not make sense to depict boundary work as taking place within neither side, neither inside the field nor outside it in another... but within the volume of a thick boundary.

Furthermore, drawing on Actor Network Theory, Eyal (2013:174) characterises boundary work as not only separating fields, but also connecting them by, 'mapping the terrain, establishing connections to who lies beyond it, transacting with them'. Eyal (2013:174) illustrates this idea with the example of the constitution of the economy, or of things as economic, which he argues,

Takes place in a boundary space between the economic field, the bureaucratic field and the academic field, by actors who have a foot in each of these, but by the same token are also somewhat marginal to each of these. What they do at once connects the economic field with the academic and bureaucratic ones – since to identify, measure, calculate and disentangle externalities, i.e. to qualify things as "economic", to produce the specific modality of activities in the field, is a collaborative effort that requires the participation of scientists, politicians, administrators, etc. – and yet reproduces their separation since the very product of this collaborative cross-boundary effort is the qualification of things and activities a "economic" or "non-economic".

Fennell (2018) also demonstrates how a boundary zone can both connect and separate fields. She argues that pole studios can reinforce differences between the field of adult entertainment and other fields by minimising outside spectatorship, restricting male participation and teaching multiple forms of pole. However, they can also connect fields by allowing the content of different pole-related classes to overlap, offering specialised classes that do not utilise a pole, for instance, or by treating poling as preparing the body for other types of specialised classes. Thus, actors occupying a boundary zone engage in boundary work that both connects and disconnects different fields.

Spaces of opportunity and hybridisation

Second, Eyal (2006, 2013) and Eyal and Pok (2011) argue that individuals and organisations positioned at the boundary of a professional field, such as journalism or humanitarianism, are under less obligation to conform to the doxa, or shared values and practices, of that field. For example, drawing on Lee's (2004) research into hybrid wellness practices, such as alternative medicine and spiritual guidance, Eyal (2013:177) argues that,

Instead of submitting to the close governmental and collegial regulation that comes with the status of professions... [actors] may choose to suspend claims for scientificity or professionalism, and remain in the space that straddles the medical field, the field of personal services, etc.

For this reason, Eyal and Pok (2011:18), describe boundary zones between fields as being 'under-regulated', or as spaces where, 'the rules about what one can legitimately do/combine are relaxed'. Instead, these boundary zones are characterised as a 'space of opportunity... a space that is underdetermined, where things can be done, combinations and conversions could be established, that are not possible to do within fields'. News organisations, for example, can position themselves at this in-between space to exploit the fact that it is under-regulated by adopting different or novel news values and role perceptions. As Eyal (2013:177) puts it, 'marginality is the mother of invention and improvisation, of seeing value in heterodox combinations and in exploiting fuzzy frontiers... There are great advantages in staying liminal'.

A key feature of the practices which might emerge in such a 'space of opportunity', according to Eyal (2013:161), is hybridity, or combinations of norms and values from multiple different fields which hold a double-meaning or "twofold truth" as Bourdieu (2000) puts it. Lee (2004:1), for example, describes 'wellness' practices as stemming from hybrid combinations of 'ideas and techniques from diverse sectors such as medicine and healing; counselling and psychotherapy; exercise and fitness; beauty and personal care services; and religion and spirituality'. However, few other studies have examined if and how such hybrid professional practices are formed in relation to actors' field position, and certainly not within journalism studies. This is unfortunate because Eyal's (2013) concepts have much potential value for the study of journalism and journalistic specialisms. For example, a recent study of entrepreneurial, constructive journalists by Wagemans, Witschge and Harbers (2019:562) concluded that these journalists,

> actively experiment and test the boundaries of what journalism is, and... that this in a way 'liberates' the entrepreneurial journalists: It allows them to break free from the naturalised and static conception of journalism that has developed over time... [It] seems to provide the journalists with a certain leeway in their practices and self-understanding.

Furthermore, Wagemans, Witschge and Harbers (2019) describe this 'leeway' as allowing entrepreneurial journalists to 'marry different, commonly-deemed incompatible practices and values, thus challenging binary distinctions at the heart of conceptualisations of journalism', such as the apparent distinction between 'stating facts' and stating solutions. However, the underlying causes of such 'liberation' are under-theorised and there is no discussion of their interaction with non-journalistic fields.

Strategic ambiguity

Third, Eyal (2013) suggests that, for actors occupying a 'thick boundary zone' between fields, it is strategically useful to maintain a degree of conceptual ambiguity when defining their practice.

> It is possible that the in-between status of the space between fields is valued for its own sake... and its fuzzy nature is therefore actively cultivated and reproduced.
>
> (Eyal 2013:177)

Specifically, Eyal and Pok (2011:19) suggest that actively reproducing 'fuzziness', or definitional vagueness, is necessary for ensuring that boundary zones remain 'spaces of opportunity' where actors can 'escape the close scrutiny and subordination that comes with entry into... [a] field'. Put simply, conceptual ambiguity is a necessary requirement for a 'space of opportunity' between fields to exist. Without it, actors would not be able to 'exploit the fact that it is an under-regulated space' (Eyal and Pok 2011:19), to produce their own novel, hybrid practices.

In one of the few empirical studies to examine this suggestion, Medvetz (2012) has shown how think tanks benefit from such 'strategic ambiguity'. He argues that think tanks thrive in the boundary zone between fields by gathering a complex mixture of forms of capital from the academic, political, economic and media fields, whilst at the same time avoiding the appearance of complete dependence on any of these institutions. This 'strategic move' or 'precarious and never-ending balancing act' is only possible, Medvetz (2012:24) suggests, if the concept of a think tank itself maintains its 'fuzziness'. Without it, think tanks would not be able to occupy their liminal field position, from which they draw great benefit. Similarly, Fennell (2018) argues that the pole studios they studied gave only vague, fleeting or imprecise references to the intended audience or venue for the practices they taught. This ambiguity was strategically useful because it enabled them to teach core pole moves based on a hybrid combination of athleticism, dance and eroticism, which allowed participants to simultaneously 'build athletic, artistic and erotic skills leverageable in various fields outside of the studios' (Fennell 2018:1965).

Is it fielded?

Both Eyal and Pok (2011) and Krause (2014) propose that boundary zones are also characterised by an absence of field-defining features which include: symbolic differentiation, field-specific symbolic capital and field-building. This argument emerges from a critical discussion of alternative ways of thinking about a 'boundary zone' – either as new fields, or as fields-in-the-making. Eyal (2013:163) suggests that the response of Bourdieu and his followers to the concept of a 'think boundary zone', would be to say that,

> We are, in fact, in no disagreement. What you call a space between fields is nothing but another field... If you are interested in marginal actors, who exist on the frontiers of fields where the lines of force become weaker, you can simply shift the focus and analyze the sphere of their activity as a different field – the field of generalized cultural production, the field of scientific popularization, the field of charity organizations, etc.

As Stampnitzky (2013:12) put it, 'many scholars have tended to apply the concept of "field" to almost everything'.

Alternatively, the kinds of individuals and organisations Fennell (2018), Stampnitzky (2013), Wagemans, Witschge and Harbers (2019) and others describe could potentially be characterised as occupying 'interstitial' fields or 'fields-in-the-making', rather than a boundary zone. Perhaps the most well documented example of an interstitial field is Medvetz's (2012) account of the field position of think tanks. He argues that these organisations thrive in the 'spaces between fields' by gathering a complex mixture of forms of capital from the academic, political, economic and media fields, whilst at the same time avoiding the appearance of complete dependence on any of these institutions. However, Medvetz (2012:25) also finds that think tanks, 'have developed certain field-like properties of their own' such as being 'ever more enmeshed in relations of "antagonistic cooperation" with one another'. As a result, he concludes that think tanks are, 'members of an interstitial field, or a semi-structured network of organizations that traverses, links, and overlaps the more established spheres of academic, political, business, and media production' (ibid).

Eyal and Pok's (2011:17) interpretation of Medvetz's (2012) analysis is slightly different. They highlight the temporary nature of the characteristics of think tanks' field position, arguing that,

> While dependent on inputs from other fields, and constrained by the need to shape output to external needs, the collective of think tanks is gradually acquiring some forms of weak autonomy; gradually becoming the site of production of specific capital and form of expertise; gradually, in short, is being made into a field.

On this basis, they suggest that think tanks are most accurately characterised as occupying a 'field-in-the-making'. Other documented 'fields-in-the-making' include the gastronomic field in 19th century France (Ferguson 1998) and the curriculum field in the US at the turn of the 20th century (Tahirsylaj 2017).

Each of these alternatives to a 'boundary zone' assumes that all areas of social life are, to at least some degree, fielded. But is this a valid assumption? Are all social practices necessarily governed by the characteristics of a field? As Krause (2014:99) explains,

> Some scholars in the Bourdieusian tradition have a tendency to assume that there are fields and to think of fields and their symbolic dimensions in static terms, but field theory provides only a starting point for further enquiry. Each field has a specific history. A given area of social life might or might not be bounded by shared assumptions, and it might or might not be shaped by competition for symbolic capital. Fields can be more or less autonomous or lose the character of 'fieldedness' altogether. Of any given area of social practice, we might thus ask; is it fielded? *Are actors oriented by each other? How is symbolic capital defined? What are the distinctions that matter among actors?*

We suggest that these three questions provide a useful basis for determining whether a sphere of social practices should be considered a 'field'. First, we can interrogate the extent to which agents in a field engage in symbolic differentiation (Krause 2017), or are 'oriented towards each other in formulating the differences' (Krause 2014:5). Indeed, it was his observations about the 'process of differentiation' between think tanks that led Medvetz (2012:38) to conclude that they were developing their own interstitial field, rather than occupying a 'boundary zone'.

> One of the main arguments of this book, in fact, will be that as think tanks have become oriented to one another in their judgements and practices, they have established a semi distinct social universe with its own logic, history, and interior structures, not to mention its own agents. It is in this historical process of differentiation that we must find the reality of the think tank. Put simply, think tanks exist as such only in so far as they have formed their own relatively stable institutional niche.

Similarly, Krause (2014) argues that humanitarian NGOs have come to inhabit a shared social space, or field, not only because they share common assumptions about what it means to be 'humanitarian', but also because they compete in a market for 'good projects' by symbolically differentiating themselves from each other. For this reason, Eyal (2013) argues that a boundary zone is likely to be characterised by a relative absence of symbolic differentiation and a 'hierarchy of worth' between actors because the social space they occupy is not fielded.

Second, a shared social space might be considered a field if the actors within it share an orientation to field-specific capital (Krause 2014). Within the humanitarian field, for example, the unique form of symbolic capital is 'humanitarian authority' (Krause 2014). This particular form of symbolic capital relies on what Fassin (2011) has termed, 'humanitarian reason', or the seemingly global moral sentiments associated with a compassionate desire to alleviate distant suffering. According to Krause (2014:124) humanitarian authority stems originally from a combination of the authority of suffering produced by war, the authority of states responsible for that suffering and the authority of the medical profession. Thus, what was once an interstitial field, overlapping the spheres of medicine and the state, has now become its own discrete, stable field, with its own unique capital. Given this, another key feature of a boundary zone, such as terrorism expertise, is that it is 'not a bounded space of its own with established boundaries and forms of "capital"' (Stampnitzky 2013:1).

Finally, social spaces require an active process of field building and institutionalisation if they are to coalesce into a discrete and bounded field (Fligstein and McAdam 2012). According to Fligstein and McAdam (2012:14), this is achieved, not only by the actions of 'incumbents' and 'challengers', as discussed earlier – but also by 'internal governance units' (IGUs). Examples of IGUs, or 'catalyst actors' (Fligstein and McAdam 2012:77), include trade associations, accrediting bodies, certification boards, ombudsmen and ethics committees. These actors, 'oversee compliance with field rules and, in general, facilitate the overall smooth functioning and reproduction of the system'. Such 'field management' legitimises and naturalises the logic and rules of the field by, for instance, collecting and providing information about the field, certifying the activities of members, liaising with actors in other fields and serving as the 'lobbying arm or 'public face' of the field (Fligstein and McAdam 2012:78). In the journalistic field, for example, the process of awarding prizes such as US Pulitzer Prizes are important internal governance mechanisms because, by rewarding certain practices over others, they help to legitimise certain norms and reproduce a professional hierarchy. Fligstein and McAdam (2012:78) also suggest that, 'the mere presence of these units... confers legitimacy on the field through the appearance of order, rationality, and equity'. By contrast, within a boundary zone, such institutional-isation is weak or absent and there are likely to be few concerted efforts at field building. In the case of terrorism expertise, for example, Stampnitzky (2013:12) argues that,

> Terrorism experts have never consolidated control over the production of either experts or knowledge. New "self-proclaimed" experts constantly emerge, no licensing body exists to certify "proper" expertise, and there is no agreement among terrorism expert about what constitutes useful knowledge. In sociological terms, the boundaries of the field are weak and permeable. There is little regulation of who may become an expert.

In summary, the final key features of a boundary zone relate to its absence of field-defining features, such as symbolic differentiation, field-specific symbolic capital and field-building.

Conclusion

In this chapter, we began by summarising key concepts within field theory – including capital, doxa and habitus – that underpin our analysis of humanitarian journalists. We then argued that, despite providing some relevant insights into the functioning of transnational, corrective and specialised forms of journalism, conventional accounts of field theory struggle to fully explain the often marginalised, hybrid norms and practices which operate at the boundaries or intersection of multiple fields. We aim to address this issue by drawing on Eyal (2006, 2013) and Eyal and Pok's (2011) corrective to field theory. It suggests that all social fields, 'secrete... thick boundary zones as an inevitable aspect of their functioning, as fuzzy zones of separation and connection' (Eyal 2013:168). Specifically, Eyal (2013) argues that the norms and practices in these social spaces are characterised by boundary work, creativity, hybridity and strategic ambiguity as well as an absence of symbolic differentiation, field-specific capital and field-building activities. We propose that humanitarian journalists are based in this boundary zone, and we use these concepts to help structure our analysis of their norms and practices. In doing so, our analysis responds to four specific sub-research questions, which we address in each of the following four chapters:

1   How do humanitarian journalists define their professional practices (Chapter 2)?

2 What news values and sourcing practices do humanitarian journalists adopt (Chapter 3)?
3 How do humanitarian journalists understand the concept of 'humanitarianism' (Chapter 4)?
4 How do humanitarian journalists relate to each other (Chapter 5)?

References

Al Yahya, K. and Fustier, N. (2011). Saudi Arabia as a Humanitarian Donor: High Potential, Little Institutionalization. First published and accessed on 17.03.2011. Available at http://dx.doi.org/10.2139/ssrn.1789163

Aneja, U. (2016). *Bold Reform or Empty Rhetoric? A Critique of the World Humanitarian Summit*. Observer Research Foundation (ORF).

Barnett, M. (2011). *Empire of Humanity: A History of Humanitarianism*. Cornell University Press.

Benson, R. and Neveu, E. (2005). *Bourdieu and the Journalistic Field*. Polity Press.

Berglez, P. (2013). *Global Journalism: Theory and Practice*. Peter Lang.

Biesla, E. (2008). The Pivotal Role of News Agencies in the Context of Globalization: A Historical Approach. *Global Networks*. 8:3. 347–366.

Bourdieu, P. (1984). *Distinction: A Social Critique of the Judgment of Taste*. Harvard University Press.

Bourdieu, P. (1993). In Johnson, R. (Ed.), *The Field of Cultural Production. Essays on Art and Literature*. Polity Press.

Bourdieu, P. (1996). *The Rules of Art: Genesis and Structure of the Literary Field*. Polity Press.

Bourdieu, P. (1998). *On Television. New Press* [trans. P. Parkhurst Ferguson].

Bourdieu, P. (2000). *Pascalian Meditations*. Stanford University Press.

Bourdieu, P. (2005). The Political Field, the Social Science Field, and the Journalistic Field. In Benson, R. and Neveu, E. (Eds.), *Bourdieu and the Journalistic Field*. Polity Press.

Bourdieu, P. and Wacquant, L. (1992). *An Invitation to Reflexive Sociology*. Polity Press.

Carlson, M. and Lewis, S. (2015). *Boundaries of Journalism: Professionalism, Practices and Participation*. Routledge.

Carroll, J. (2006). *Foreign News Coverage: The U.S. Media's Undervalued Asset*. Joan Shorenstein Center on the Press, Politics and Public Policy Working Paper Series.

Champagne, P. (1993). The View from the Media. In Bourdieu, P. et al. (Eds.), *The Weight of the World*. Polity Press.

Champagne, P. (2005). The Double Dependency: The Journalistic Field Between Politics and Markets – Patrick Champagne. In Benson, R. and Neveu, E. (Eds.), *Bourdieu and the Journalistic Field*. Polity Press. 48–64.

Christin, A. (2016). Is Journalism a Transnational Field? Asymmetrical Relations and Symbolic Domination in Online News. *The Sociological Review*. 64:2. 212–234.

Couldry, N. (2003). Media Meta-Capital: Extending the Range of Bourdieu's Field Theory. *Theory and Society.* 32. 653–677.

Denĉik, L. (2013). What Global Citizens and Whose Global Moral Order? Defining the Global at BBC World News. *Global Media and Communication.* 9:2. 119–134.

Derbal, N. (2022). Humanitarian and Relief Organisations in Global South Da'awa. In Mandaville, P. (Ed.), *Wahhabism and the World: Understanding Saudi Arabia's Global Influence on Islam.* Open University Press.

Dickenson, R. (2008). Studying the Sociology of Journalists: The Journalistic Field and the New World. *Sociology Compass.* 2:5. 1383–1399.

Domatob, J. K. and Hall, S. W. (1983). Development Journalism in Black Africa. *International Communication Gazette.* 31. 9–33.

Duval, J. (2005). Economic Journalism in France. In Benson, R. and Neveu, E. (Eds.), *Bourdieu and the Journalistic Field.* Polity Press.

Eldridge, S. (2018). *Online Journalism from the Periphery: Interloper Media and the Journalistic Field.* Routledge.

English, P. (2015). Mapping the Sports Journalism Field: Bourdieu and Broadsheet Newsrooms. *Journalism.* 7:8. 1001–1017.

Eyal, G. (2006). *The Disenchantment of the Orient: Expertise in Arab Affairs and the Israeli State.* Stanford University Press.

Eyal, G. (2013). Spaces between Fields. In Gorski, P. (Ed.), *Bourdieu and Historical Analysis.* Duke University Press. 158–182.

Eyal, G. and Pok, G. (2011). From a Sociology of Professions to a Sociology of Expertise. *Expert Determination Electronic Law Journal.* http://exp ertdeterminationelectroniclawjournal.com/eyal-g-and-pok-g-2013-from-a-sociology-of-professions-to-a-sociology-of-expertise/

Fassin, D. (2011). *Humanitarian Reason: A Moral History of the Present.* University of California Press.

Fennell, D. (2018). Pole Studios as Spaces Between the Adult Entertainment, Art, Fitness and Sporting Fields. *Sport and Society.* 21:12. 1957–1973.

Ferguson, P. P. (1998). A Cultural Field in the Making: Gastronomy in 19th-Century France. *American Journal of Sociology.* 104:3. 597–641.

Ferron, B., Kotišová, J. and Smith, S. (2022). The Primacy of Secondary Things: A Sustained Scientific Dialogue on Three Edges of the Journalistic Field. *Journal Media.* 3. 212–227.

Figenschou, T. U. (2011). Suffering Up Close: The Strategic Construction of Mediated Suffering on Al Jazeera English. *International Journal of Communication.* 5. 233–253.

Fligstein, N. and McAdam, M. (2012). *A Theory of Fields.* Oxford University Press.

Galtung, J. (2003). Peace Journalism. *Media Asia.* 30:3. 177–180.

Ghanem, Y. (2021). *Al Jazeera, Freedom of the Press and Forecasting Humanitarian Emergencies.* Routledge.

Gieryn, T. (1983). Boundary-Work and the Demarcation of Science from Non-Science: Strains and Interests in Professional Ideologies of Scientists. *American Sociological Review.* 48:6. 781–795.

Gong, L. (2021). Humanitarian Diplomacy as an Instrument for China's Image-Building. *Asian Journal of Comparative Politics.* 6:3. 238–252.

Hallin, D. (2005). Two Approaches to Comparative Media Research: Field Theory and Differentiation Theory. In Benson, R. and Neveu, E. (Eds.), *Bourdieu and the Journalistic Field.* Polity Press.

Hesmondhaulgh, D. (2006). Bourdieu, the Media and Cultural Production. *Media, Culture and Society.* 28:2. 211–231.

Horvit, B. (2006). International News Agencies and the War Debate of 2003. *International Communication Gazette.* 68:5–6. 427–447.

Hovden, J. (2001). The Norwegian Journalistic Field. Issues and Problems in an Ongoing Research Project. In *15th Nordic Conference on Media and Communication Research.* Reykjavik, 11–13 August 2001: Jan Fredrik Hovden. Department of Media and Journalism. Volda University College. Norway.

Krause, M. (2014). *The Good Project: Humanitarian Relief NGOs and the Fragmentation of Reason.* University of Chicago Press.

Krause, M. (2017). How Fields Vary. *British Journal of Sociology.* 69:1. 3–22.

Krebs, H. B. (2016). The Changing Role of China in International Humanitarian Cooperation: Challenges and Opportunities. In Heins, V. M., Koddenbrock, K. and Unrau, C. (Eds.), *Humanitarianism and Challenges of Cooperation.* Routledge.

Lee, J. (2004). Investigating the Hybridity of 'Wellness' Practices. Theory and Research in Comparative Social Analysis.

Lynch, J. and McGoldrick, A. (2005). *Peace Journalism.* Hawthorn Press.

Maares, P. and Hanusch, F. (2020). Interpretations of the Journalistic Field: A Systematic Analysis of How Journalism Scholarship Appropriates Bourdieusian Thought. *Journalism.* 23:4. 736–754.

Marchetti, D. (2005). Subfields of Specialised Journalism. In Benson, R. and Neveu, E. (Eds.), *Bourdieu and the Journalistic Field.* Polity Press.

Markham, T. (2011). The Political Phenomenology of War Reporting. *Journalism.* 12:5. 567–585.

Maurer, P. (2014). Humanitarian Diplomacy and Principled Humanitarian Action. Speech given by Mr Peter Maurer, President of the International Committee of the Red Cross, Maison de la Paix, Geneva, 2 October 2014. International Review of the Red Cross.

McBride, S. (1980). *One World, Many Voices.* UNESCO.

McIntyre, K. (2019). Solutions Journalism. *Journalism Practice.* 13:1. 16–34.

McIntyre, K. and Lough. K. (2021). Toward a Clearer Conceptualization and Operationalization of Solutions Journalism. *Journalism.* 22:6.

Medvetz, T. (2012). *Think Tanks in America.* University of Chicago Press.

Mellor, N. (2008). Arab Journalists as Cultural Intermediaries. *The International Journal of Press/Politics.* 13. 465–483.

Miles, H. (2005). *Al-Jazeera: How Arab TV News Changed the World.* Abacus.

Moussa, J. (2014). *Ancient Origins, Modern Actors: Defining Arabic Meanings of Humanitarianism.* Oversees Development Institute.

Neveu, E. (2007). Pierre Bourdieu: Sociologist of Media, or Sociologist for Media Scholars? *Journalism Studies.* 8:2. 335–347.

Örnebring, H., Karlsson, M., Fast, K. and Lindell, J. (2018). The Space of Journalistic Work – A Theoretical Model. *Communication Theory*. 28:4. 403–423.

Painter, J. (2008). *Counter-Hegemonic News: A Case Study of Al-Jazeera English and Telesûr*. Reuters Institute for the Study of Journalism. University of Oxford.

Powers, M. (2015). NGOs as Journalistic Entities: The Possibilities, Promises and Limits of Boundary Crossing. In Carlson, M. and Lewis, S. (Eds.), *Boundaries of Journalism: Professionalism, Practices and Participation*. Routledge. 186–201.

Sambrook, R. (2010). *Are Foreign Correspondents Redundant?* Reuters.

Schapals, A. K. (2022). *Peripheral Actors in Journalism: Deviating from the Norm?* Routledge.

Schultz, I. (2007). The Journalistic Gut Feeling. *Journalism Practice*. 1:2. 190–207.

Schudson, M. (2005). Autonomy from What? In Benson, R. and Neveu, E. (Eds.), *Bourdieu and the Journalistic Field*. Polity Press.

Shaw, I. S. and Selvarajah, S. (Eds.). (2019). *Reporting Human Rights, Conflicts, and Peacebuilding: Critical and Global Perspectives*. Palgrave Macmillan.

Stampnitzky, L. (2011). Disciplining an Unruly Field: Terrorism Experts and Theories of Scientific/Intellectual Production. *Qualitative Sociology*. 34:1. 1–19.

Stampnitzky, L. (2013). *Disciplining Terrorism: How Experts Invented Terrorism*. Cambridge University Press.

Swartz, D. (1998). *Culture and Power: The Sociology of Pierre Bourdieu*. Chicago University Press.

Tahirsylaj, A. (2017). Curriculum Field in the Making: Influences That Led to Social Efficiency as Dominant Curriculum Ideology in Progressive Era in the U.S. *European Journal of Curriculum Studies*. 4:1. 618–628.

Thussu, D. (2000). Legitimizing Humanitarian Intervention? CNN, NATO and the Kosovo Crisis. *European Journal of Communication*. 15:3. 345–361.

Tunstall, J. (1971). *Journalists at Work*. Constable.

Van Leuven, S. and Berglez, P. (2016). Global Journalism between Dream and Reality: A Comparative Study of the Times, Le Monde and De Standaard. *Journalism Studies*. 17:6. 667–683.

Wacquant, L. (1989). Towards a Reflexive Sociology: A Workshop with Pierre Bourdieu. *Sociological Theory*. 7:1. 26–63.

Wagemans, A., Witschge, T. and Harbers, F. (2019). Impact as Driving Force of Journalistic and Social Change. *Journalism: Theory, Practice and Criticism*. 20:4. 552–567.

Webb, J. et al. (Eds.). (2002). *Understanding Bourdieu*. Allen and Unwin.

Williams, K. (2011). *International Journalism*. Sage.

Wright, K. (2015). "These Grey Areas" How and Why Freelance Work Blurs INGOs and News Organizations. *Journalism Studies*. 17:8. 989–1009.

Wright, K. (2016). Moral Economies: Interrogating the Interactions of NGOs, Journalists and Freelancers. *International Journal of Communication*. 10. 1510–1529.

Wright, K. (2018). *Who's Reporting Africa Now? Non-Governmental Organizations, Journalists and Multimedia*. Peter Lang.

Xiaoge, X. (2009). Development Journalism. In Wahl-Jorgensen, K. and Hanitzsch, Y. (Eds.), *The Handbook of Journalism Studies*. Routledge. 357–370.

2   Insiders and outsiders
Peripheral, precarious and constructive watchdogs

In this chapter, we ask – how do humanitarian journalists describe themselves and their work? Do they consider themselves to be journalists, humanitarians, both, or neither? What kinds of journalists and/or humanitarians do they see themselves as, and how do they distinguish themselves from other professionals in these – and other – fields? What implications does such 'boundary work' have for their status, financial security and professional practices?

We begin by arguing that humanitarian journalists simultaneously connect and disconnect the fields of journalism and humanitarianism, just as Eyal (2013) predicts of actors operating at the 'boundary zone' between different fields. They describe themselves as journalists but not mainstream journalists, for example, and as humanitarians but 'more objective' than aid agency communicators. As Francesca (2014) put it, they 'play... both sides; acting as insider and outsider at the same time'.

We go on to demonstrate that this role leaves humanitarian journalists as peripheral actors in both fields. As a result, they generally lack the status of most journalistic and humanitarian actors, and can suffer significant financial insecurity. This position is linked to their role perceptions. These journalists want to 'make a difference' – but without being seen as 'advocates', since this would compromise both their journalistic and humanitarian norms. Perhaps most significantly, their peripheral field position and combination of journalistic and humanitarian norms generally leads them to adopt the role of constructive, rather than severely critical, watchdogs – though there are exceptions.

Separating fields

Most of the 30 humanitarian journalists in our core sample defined themselves – at least partly – in relation to the subject matter they

DOI: 10.4324/9781003356806-3

covered. These thematic 'beats' included 'aid', 'crises', global development, global health, humanitarianism, malnutrition, refugees and 'the world's biggest problems'. However, when describing their professional practices, or *how* they covered these subjects, these journalists and the news outlets they worked for often avoided the question. Instead, they characterised themselves and their practices through a process of differentiation, or by distinguishing themselves from various fields of practice. For example, in its 2016 annual report, The New Humanitarian (TNH) described itself as, 'faster than think tanks, more accessible than academic journals, more objective than aid agency communications, and more consistent and in-depth than mainstream media'. In doing so, TNH presented itself as at least partly separate from the fields of academia, humanitarianism, journalism and the liminal field occupied by think tanks (see Medvetz 2012). In fact, this 'elaborate game of differentiation' (Medvetz 2012:44) appears to mirror the way think tanks present themselves. Medvetz's (2012:131) argues that 'a think tank must demonstrate that it is not a lobbying firm, a university, a business, an advocacy group and so on. To do so, it must simply highlight its differences from these organizations'.

When defining their practices, humanitarian journalists and the news outlets they worked for compared themselves most often to actors in the fields of journalism and humanitarianism. For example, in explaining its 'mission' Humanosphere warned its readers: 'don't be surprised if what you get at Humanosphere is a bit different from what you'd get from the mainstream media'. Specifically, it described itself as seeking to not only 'fill in for the dearth of mainstream media coverage of humanitarian issues' but also provide an alternative to the 'traditional narrative on aid and development [that] is frequently weak, predictable and boring'. At the same time, Humanosphere also defined itself in opposition to aid agency communications which, it argued, have a 'tendency to produce simple, promotional messages that avoid difficult, politically charged or awkward issues'.

Such rhetorical 'boundary work', or acts of professional differentiation (Gieryn 1983), was even more common amongst our interviewees, who repeatedly defined their professional practices in contrast to both 'mainstream' journalism and institutionalised humanitarian communication. For example, in the following quotation, one respondent described their 'nuanced' but 'accessible' reporting practices as striking a 'balance' between the 'very simplified' reporting of 'normal' news outlets and the 'dense' or 'patronising' communications from humanitarian organisations.

Because of fundraising, humanitarian organisations simplify the messages enormously, and present a very undignified, patronising image of people in distress... giving the impression that, as humanitarians, we can just go out and save people... Being able to explain those complexities and those nuances in a way that is accessible is very, very important. The newspapers don't do that [either]. They put out a very simplified version. It can't be as dense as an Overseas Development Institute report! [Laughs] It must be easier, more immediate, more reader-friendly, but there is a balance to be struck and I think we do that a lot better than normal news agencies, broadcasters, or broadsheets.

The most frequently made comparisons were with the professional practices of 'mainstream' journalists and news outlets. As one respondent put it, 'what we are writing is something they can't get in the mainstream media'. Another said that they found their current work 'attractive' because 'it allowed for a kind of journalism that was harder and harder to accommodate in other news outlets'. This alternative 'kind of journalism' was defined largely in terms of its distinct news values and sourcing practices – as we explain in more detail in Chapter 3.

When comparing their professional practices with those in the humanitarian field, respondents repeatedly referred to the apparent 'censorship' or 'limitations on editorial independence' and focus on 'positive' stories, which, they argued, characterised institutionalised humanitarian communication. As one respondent put it, 'I just feel that, as a journalist working in this area, you should be challenging companies rather than doing their press relations for them'. Another interviewee told us that,

If it is in the field of promotional cheerleading for various non-profit causes, then that is not our vision. That would probably start to cross the line for us. As long as its something in the field of journalism... If it is independent journalism of some kind, then we are cool.

In summary, humanitarian journalists appeared to define their practices, in part, by describing what they were not, or by distancing themselves especially from 'mainstream' journalistic and humanitarian practices. Put another way, boundary work was central to their professional identities.

Connecting fields

Eyal (2013) argues that such boundary work cannot, logically, take place within a field, since the act of producing distinctions between fields is not itself an institutionalised professional practice (as explained in Chapter 2). Instead, he argues that boundary work must take place at the site of the 'boundary zone' *between* fields. However, a boundary zone does not only separate or distinguish what is inside and outside of a field. It is also, according to Eyal (2013:163), 'where networks provide for a seamless connection between fields', since boundary work requires a 'collaborative cross-boundary effort'. For this reason, Eyal (2013:163) argues that actors within the boundary are simultaneously excluded from the field *and* important actors who influence the field, because they play a network role.

The idea that actors who define their practice in part through boundary work not only separate fields, but also connect them, is clear in the way humanitarian journalists – and many of the news outlets they work for – described their practice. If we re-examine the forms of self-presentation given above, we can find evidence that each disconnection from a field also simultaneously establishes a connection with another. For example, by describing itself as '*faster* than think tanks, *more accessible* than academic journals and *more objective* than aid agency communications', TNH references professional values associated with the journalistic field, including timeliness, accessibility and objectivity. At the same time, by describing itself as '*more consistent and in-depth* than mainstream media', TNH identifies with practices associated with the production of communication within the humanitarian field. As Medvetz (2012:44) put it, 'each seeming act of separation is built on a corresponding strategy of affiliation'.

Similarly, to distinguish itself from 'mainstream' journalism that is often 'weak, predictable and boring', Humanosphere described itself as having 'a commitment to making the world a better place' and a 'desire to reduce poverty and injustice around the world'. In doing so, it drew explicitly on norms from the humanitarian field. Equally, to distance itself from institutional humanitarian communications, which 'have a tendency to produce simple, promotional messages', Humanosphere described itself as tackling issues that are, 'difficult, politically charged and awkward... [since] that's where you find the best stories'. In the process, it drew on journalistic norms of storytelling and pursuing accountability.

Interviewees' characterisations of their professional practices also highlighted a simultaneous connection and separation from the journalistic and humanitarian fields. For example, in the process of comparing their practices with those of aid agencies, which allegedly 'censor the real humanitarian situation', the testimonies cited above highlight the importance of autonomy and of an ability to critique the aid sector. In doing so, they draw directly on journalistic norms associated with independence and acting as a 'watchdog'. Similarly, when criticising 'mainstream' journalism for being insufficiently concerned with the outcomes or impact of their journalism, our respondents regularly drew on the humanitarian principle of alleviating suffering. This is made clear when interviewees spoke instead, of having an 'objective to improve people's lives... through journalism', for example, or more generally, of an alternative 'desire to be constructive with our journalism... while adhering to all standard journalism ethics and standards', and to produce 'good journalism that has impact'.

Yet, as these quotations also illustrate, humanitarian journalists never rejected the label of 'journalist', despite partly defining themselves in opposition to 'mainstream' journalism. Instead, they repeatedly characterised themselves as adopting a different 'kind' of journalism, that they 'believed in' or were more 'passionate about'. As one interviewee explained, 'even though we manifest it differently... we all feel like we're doing a special kind of journalism that is increasingly rare, and that we're fighting to keep it alive'. The specialist news outlets they often worked for were also keen to highlight their journalistic credentials. News Deeply, for example, described itself as providing, 'rigorous reporting and analysis... meeting high standards... with dedication and integrity... producing the opposite of fake news'. Its tagline in 2018 was 'quality journalism for our troubled times'.

On occasion, some respondents and news outlets even described themselves explicitly as connecting both humanitarian and journalistic practices. For example, one interviewee told us that, 'I decided to take this job... [to] be able to link up everything that I knew from the field, from the development sector, from the humanitarian sector, into what this [news] organisation does'. Similarly, Humanosphere described itself as 'an independent, non-profit news site that gives a damn'. In an earlier version of their editorial strategy, one news outlet even stated explicitly that, 'we occupy a unique space at the intersection of news media and humanitarian policy and practice'.

In summary, when defining their professional identities, the humanitarian journalists in our sample and many of the specialist news outlets that employed them described themselves as both inside and outside the humanitarian and journalistic fields – just as Eyal (2013) predicts. This simultaneous connection and distancing from the journalist field also explains why our respondents compared them-selves with *'mainstream'* journalism, rather than with journalism in general. This terminology enables humanitarian journalists to retain the label of 'journalist', whilst also identifying a contrasting journalis-tic 'other'. By contrast, since the term 'humanitarian' is generally not used exclusively to describe professional actors within the humani-tarian field (in the same way that the label of 'journalist' is a more definitive 'boundary marker' within the journalistic field) it was not necessary for respondents to compare themselves with 'mainstream' humanitarians.

In most cases, maintaining this dual position of insiders and outsid-ers of the fields of both journalism and humanitarianism did not cause obvious contradictions because both fields were understood to share a number of similar values. As one respondent told us,

> there are a lot of things in the ethical code of humanitarians that would also be true to journalists. Very simple things like inde-pendence, neutrality, and impartiality. Those things are not just for Reuters, but also for the Red Cross.

However, there were some tensions regarding humanitarian journal-ists' role perceptions. In line with dominant journalistic norms regard-ing impartiality, and norms regarding political neutrality within the 'chemical' tradition of humanitarianism (Orgad 2013), most human-itarian journalists were not willing to become advocates in order to 'make a difference'. As one interviewee put it, 'in the past, before I became a journalist, I worked in advocacy... But [I'm] on this side of the fence now'. Another said, 'I think there is a line between journal-istic storytelling and advocacy, and we try to really be very mindful of that line'. Given that 'advocacy' is widely regarding as an important 'boundary marker' for determining who is inside or outside the jour-nalistic field (Singer 2015), adopting this identity would have severely compromised humanitarian journalistic credibility. Indeed, most of the journalists we spoke to within our wider study, who adhered more closely to conventional professional norms of journalistic impartiality and detachment, generally rejected the idea that they were seeking to achieve any specific outcomes, arguing instead that, 'I'm not trying to achieve anything'.

Despite this, some humanitarian journalists struggled to reconcile this stance with their goal of exposing and explaining the structural causes of suffering, which falls within the 'alchemical' tradition of hu-manitarianism (Orgad 2013). As one interviewee put it, 'I am not in journalism for vanity's sake. I want to make an actual difference in the lives of people around the world'. This tension often led to more mixed or even contradictory role perceptions, as in the following quotation:

> I wouldn't say we are advocates... It is not necessarily a specific outcome that I am looking for. Although, broadly speaking, our goal is to address the issue of malnutrition and to reduce it, so I guess there is that advocacy component to it.

Another interviewee described themselves as operating at the 'blurred lines between activism and journalism'.

Peripheral actors

There was a cost to this ambiguous balancing act for the humanitarian journalists in our study: it meant they were peripheral actors in both fields. This marginal position was illustrated in several ways. For some, it was reflected in the degree of 'caution' they expressed when assuming the label of 'journalist'. As one interviewee told us,

> We are perhaps a little careful not to overstate our journalism with a capital 'J'... I'm cautious about claiming the mantle of journalism... Our product... I think qualifies as journalism... [But] there is a little inferiority, just a caution, to say what we do is a kind of journalism.

Other interviewees suggested that their professional practices could only be defined as 'journalistic' if they adopted a relatively broad understanding of the term. As the following quotation reveals, they often stated that the key criteria for qualifying as a journalist was to produce content that fulfilled a public service, in some way.

> I think our work was less tied to a news agenda, but it was still, overall, journalism in the sense that it was informing a public of something that they might not know, with some kind of public service utility goal and still timely in a longer time-frame period.

Similarly, another interviewee explained, 'in the broader sense, journalism is a public service... At its very best, journalism serves the public, so that is what we are doing'.

Finally, some interviewees told us that they only considered certain aspects of their professional practices to be journalistic. For example, one said that, despite routinely carrying out some tasks which she considered non-journalistic, 'we know that we are, at the core, journalists'. In each case, these individuals appear to acknowledge that there are limits to what can be considered 'journalism' and that their professional practices are near to those limits. As one respondent put it, 'I would still categorise [what we produce] as news but on one end of the scale'. By describing themselves in this way, the humanitarian journalists in our study positioned themselves at a distance away from the centre or core of the journalistic field, or as further away from its autonomous pole.

A space of marginalisation

Because they occupy a peripheral position, humanitarian journalists may struggle to obtain prestige and recognition in either the humanitarian or journalistic field (Fligstein and McAdam 2012). Interviewees articulated this concern in several ways. A number of respondents spoke about their desire to have more 'respect' from other journalists and the limits of the journalistic 'reputation' of the specialist news outlets they worked for. In the following quotation, for example, one interviewee explains how 'other journalists... dismiss' her coverage of humanitarian issues, engaging in boundary work themselves.

> Some people look at my reporting and say, 'Oh, there's an activism element to it'. It's used as a dismissive term most of the time, like, 'Oh, you're an activist rather than journalist'. I just think that is used as a tactic to dismiss coverage of humanitarian issues, if I am honest. It is like, 'if you're covering a humanitarian issue, that is something for an activist, rather than a journalist'. That, to me, is crazy. Just because we are not covering some intensely dry policy and we are looking at these broader human rights abuses, and trying to report on that. Most of the time that dismissive attitude comes from other journalists.

Similarly, several interviewees complained about receiving insufficient credit or recognition from other journalists for their work. As one respondent lamented,

> Being early consistently drives us mad. You can only do so much prediction. The coups in Burkina [Faso]. The Nepal earthquake. A potential famine in Yemen. We are consistently ahead but no one knows it. There isn't much reward for being early except bragging

rights. If you ask enough journalists, they will acknowledge [they] get useful background from us. But there isn't much reward for being early.

Indeed, when speaking to communications officers working for INGOs and UN agencies, as part of our wider research, they regularly suggested that news coverage by specialist news outlets was less likely to be taken seriously than similar reporting by more mainstream news organisations. This was most obvious in discussion about investigative reporting. For example, in a conversation about a New York Times investigation into the UN's relationship with the Syrian regime, two communications officers claimed that, 'if [a specialist news outlet] had done that article on Syria... we'd have just discredited them'.

According to Örnebring et al. (2018), journalistic capital not only gives prestige in the journalistic field, but it also has material consequences. For our respondents, the most frequently discussed implication of a relative lack of journalistic capital was a persistent difficulty in gaining access to sources. Several interviewees described how the lack of 'name recognition' or 'cache' of their news outlet made much more difficult for them to access 'top-level government sources' compared to news producers working for more established, or larger news outlets. One editor described this as a form of 'discrimination' whereby, 'there are certain people who won't talk to small media houses'. Several interviewees also suggested that the relative lack of journalistic capital held by their news outlet affected staff recruitment. They argued that improving the 'presence', 'brand' and 'name' of their organisation would enable them to 'recruit some really good talent', and 'have a stronger team'.

Economic consequences

This relative lack of journalistic capital also exacerbates the challenges specialist non-profit news outlets generally face in attracting advertisers, reader revenues and most other forms of financial support. Like most journalists working for news non-profits, many interviewees described themselves as, 'having to prove ourselves, make a name for ourselves to attract more funding and to attract the following we need to get the funding'. However, establishing a strong reputation was made more difficult by the challenge to their credibility.

For this reason, most interviewees described their news outlet as being 'plagued by funding crises'. As one Director told us, 'it's a matter of survival, but we are holding on and we have cut everything down to the minimum in terms of staff and salary... Last year was really bad... How we survive is an absolute miracle'. In fact, during our research, financial difficulties forced several outlets we were studying to either dramatically downsize or close permanently. In July 2016, SciDev.Net announced that it was cutting 90% of its London staff, including the whole London editorial team, due to insufficient funding.[1] In July 2017, Humanosphere was forced to 'hibernate', citing 'a loss of funding and difficulty in attracting new financial backers'. It never re-opened. In June 2019, BRIGHT magazine 'closed its doors' because, 'grant money dwindled'.

Even those news outlets which did survive were generally described as having 'greatly reduced resources', relative to the 'mainstream' news outlets they often compared themselves to.[2] As one journalist put it, 'no one's got any money and there's a limit to what can be reported on... [especially] resource-intense, long-form... deeply-reported pieces from the field'. This lack of economic capital also effected journalists' salaries, financial security and working conditions (see Örnebring et al. 2018). In this respect, interviewees spoke of being 'always short-staffed', not having 'a salary matching the market rate', needing to have 'another source of income', an absence of 'steady money' and 'paid leave... if your child's sick' and in some cases, simply not having 'been paid for a while'.

Those news outlets which were able to survive did so because they received funding from a small number of bi-lateral donors (including Canada, Sweden and Switzerland) and/or private foundations (especially the Bill and Melinda Gates Foundation) who valued the combination of journalistic and humanitarian capital these organisations produced. For example, one government donor told us that they supported TNH because it has a 'specialised understanding of humanitarianism, in the way that other journalism doesn't' but also because it produces 'high-quality stuff... [that] feeds into a lot of media' and 'gets the public's attention'.

Interestingly, some humanitarian actors, which cross-subsidised humanitarian journalism as part of their wider operations, appeared to consider journalistic capital particularly valuable within the humanitarian field because of its association with 'independence'. One interviewee argued that despite being a financial 'drain', supporting humanitarian journalism was important for adding 'legitimacy to the other aspects of our [organisation]'. Another described their 'independent news service' as providing 'soft power' or 'brand-enhancing equity value' to the organisation.

However, the amount of money any of these donors allocated to humanitarian journalism was, as one donor representative put it 'very little'. Another described it as, 'a tiny, miserable amount of money'. Furthermore, in general, very few donors valued this combination of journalistic and humanitarian capital and/or were willing to support organisations with less journalistic and/or humanitarian capital than other potential grantees. For example, for most government aid agencies and foundations seeking to support humanitarian assistance, the actions of the news outlets in our sample were not sufficiently able to demonstrate their direct impact on these objectives. This was the main reason why the UK's former Department for International Development (DFID) stopped providing support for development awareness in the media. A review of its work in this area concluded that, 'the link between these programmes and poverty reduction is not strong enough to satisfy our rigorous criteria for development impact' (Dominy et al. 2011:2).[3]

Likewise, for foundations without such instrumentalist objectives, which sought to support media freedom per se, by funding journalistic capacity building activities, the news outlets in our study were often judged to have insufficient audience reach, trust or engagement – or other signs of journalistic 'quality'. In short, for them, humanitarian journalists often did not have sufficient journalistic capital. Moreover, even if they did, they still had to compete with all other journalistic actors for such funding (Scott, Wright and Bunce 2018). Thus, their marginal field position helps to explain why humanitarian journalists are generally financially insecure.

Even when the news outlets in our study were able to secure relevant bilateral or foundation-funding, such financial support was not without its challenges. Given the small number of active donors in this area, the news outlets in our sample were very vulnerable to sudden changes in their strategies or priorities. For a time, News Deeply appeared to buck this trend. Since establishing its first single-issue news site – Syria Deeply – in 2012, it grew rapidly – adding six other single-issue sites to its portfolio over the next six years, thanks to support from several different foundations. However, in September 2018, News Deeply 'paused work' on most of their platforms, including Oceans Deeply, Malnutrition Deeply and Peacebuilding Deeply because 'financial support for the platforms has come to a close'.[4]

We have also argued elsewhere that foundation funding for international non-profit news outlets can inadvertently shape the *boundaries* of such journalism, or how journalists understand, value and practice their work (Scott, Bunce and Wright 2019). Specifically, we argued that foundations direct humanitarian journalists – both intentionally and unintentionally – towards more outcome-oriented, longer-form, off-agenda coverage in a small number of niche subject areas, which broadly aligned with the priorities of the most active foundations. Furthermore, because of these changes, non-profit news outlets are incentivised to employ new, non-editorial staff and devote more time to non-editorial activities such as administration and marketing, leaving less time to produce news content.

Humanitarian journalists' dependence on a small number of private foundations can also makes them vulnerable to wealthy individuals, who are alleged to have been involved in illegal or unethical dealings, to use the financial support of a worthy cause as form of 'moral window-dressing' (Koehn and Ueng 2010, quoted in Wright et al. 2019:679). Indeed, one of the most difficult cases we came across involved TNH's attempts to deal with the increasingly serious and frequent allegations that its main donor at the time, Jho Low, played a central role in the embezzlement of billions of dollars from a development bank known as 1MDB in Malaysia (Wright et al. 2019). TNH parted company from Low at the end of 2015: Low is still a fugitive, who is wanted in multiple jurisdictions.

But perhaps the greatest concern regarding donor funding is the potential threat to journalistic autonomy (Benson 2017; Schiffrin 2017; Wright, Scott and Bunce 2020; Örnebring and Karlsson 2022). Within field theory, actors at the periphery of a social field are understood to be more vulnerable to 'capture' (Schiffrin 2021), or domination by external forces, because they have a relative lack of field-specific capital and associated autonomy (Fligstein and McAdam 2012). There was evidence of this amongst some, but certainly not all, of our interviewees. For example, one respondent admitted to regularly receiving and acting on suggestions from a funder for 'interesting stories' and people to 'speak to'. Humanitarian journalist's peripheral field position appeared to make it particularly difficult to 'write bluntly about aid while you're also courting donor funding', as one respondent put it. Similarly, another interviewee told us,

> There is no doubt that there is a pressure, subtle and sometimes not subtle, to do stories or to follow stories or to at least pay lip service to stories that relate, in some ways, to the good work being done by industry groups.

In the most extreme case, one interviewee admitted to historical experiences of direct censorship from a foundation when trying to write critically about the aid sector.

However, a pressure to write more positively and to refrain from pursuing conventional 'watchdog' journalism did not just derive from the pursuit and maintenance of donor funding. Several interviewees noted that their proximity to the humanitarian field meant they were not only broadly supportive of it, but also that they shared the humanitarian principle of 'do no harm' – both of which encouraged them to write more constructively than critically. As one journalist explained, 'I went into this, as a journalist, thinking, 'I am going to make these people accountable', but, at the same time, I have come to realise I don't want to undermine organisations that are fundamentally trying to do the right thing'. Consequently, some interviewees admitted that they had previously, 'pulled their punches', written 'quite softish leads on the story', or 'talked about opportunities for learning lessons, rather than cock-ups'. We have characterised this previously as assuming the role of a *constructive* watchdog (Scott, Bunce and Wright 2017). As one interviewee explained,

> I would say there is a way to be constructive while being a watchdog... There is a conscious effort to be critical, but also look at how that criticism could really feed into the conversation rather than take away from it.

Interestingly, one interviewee commented that, after reducing their reliance on funding from humanitarian actors, they 'have more distance now.... [and] I think that has opened up space for us to do some more investigative journalism'. It is also worth noting the larger news outlets in our sample, which were able to maintain a relatively diverse revenue stream, have been able to consistently produce critical investigative journalism about the humanitarian aid sector. For example, in recent years, TNH have exposed instances of corruption and system failures within the humanitarian sector, including financial and sex abuse scandals within the United Nations and international NGOs.

Despite some evidence of direct and indirect donor influence, in most cases, humanitarian journalists claimed to be unwilling to accept funding or other support from private foundations or aid organisations that might compromise (or be perceived to compromise) their editorial independence in any way. Respondents gave numerous examples of offers of financial support from donors which had been rejected – even when this risked or resulted in the closure of their organisation. For example, in her final article for Bright Magazine before it closed, the editor wrote that she 'chose to say no to the few offers of money I received' even though it would have enabled it to keep BRIGHT running – because,

I wanted to build a space that freely questioned the norms and culture of the international development sector, and I worried that if we began to take PR and communications money, our hands would get tied down (even though every potential funder I met promised us editorial independence).

Indeed, every donor we spoke to said they fully understood the need to protect their grantee's autonomy. As a representative of one private foundation told us,

I am concerned about making sure that we aren't doing damage to that entity in pursuit of our own goals and objectives … I want to make sure we are engaging them in the right way, so the independence remains.

We have argued elsewhere that the most active foundations in this area regard it as being in their interests to maintain the autonomy of their grantees as otherwise the impact of the reporting they support would be undermined (see Scott, Bunce and Wright 2019). As an interviewee working for News Deeply commented,

Our funders have been exceptionally clear that they do not want to direct the coverage… because they know that true value is in us providing exceptional quality journalism that is credible. That has currency, because no one questions it… because, frankly, paid content is not respected… [and is] viewed as somewhat tinged.

As a result, compromising – or being perceived to compromise – a news organisations' editorial decision-making would be counter-productive because it would undermine journalism's epistemic authority, which foundations rely upon to achieve their objectives. Being seen to protect grantees' autonomy was also important for avoiding potential flak from critics of philanthro-journalism, who might accuse foundations of 'tainting' journalistic objectivity.

Conclusion

In summary, humanitarian journalists claimed to produce an alternative *kind* of journalism, which simultaneously connects and disconnects the fields of humanitarianism and journalism. In doing so, however, they positioned themselves at the periphery of both fields, with consequences for their credibility and professional practice.

Being connected to both fields did allow humanitarian journalists to claim a degree of journalistic and humanitarian authority. However, few potential funders value this combination of humanitarian and journalistic symbolic capital, leaving almost all the news outlets in our study very financially insecure. This undermined their working conditions considerably. For this reason, we characterise the 'boundary zone' that humanitarian journalists occupied as a 'space of marginalisation'.

Despite this, the implications for their autonomy and watchdog function were not what you might expect. Their peripheral field position suggests that they should be particularly vulnerable to donor 'capture'. However, they intentionally chose to position themselves at the periphery of the humanitarian field, to retain greater autonomy from it and the humanitarian donors which did fund them valued their work precisely because of their association with journalistic independence. As a result, humanitarian journalists appear to be less susceptible to 'capture' than their peripheral field position suggests. However, this may also help to explain why there are so few humanitarian journalists – because they would rather quit than be 'captured'.

Similarly, their chronic lack of financial security suggests that these news organisations might be reluctant to criticise potential funders. However, their relatively outcome-oriented role perceptions and intentional positioning at the periphery of the humanitarian field meant they did still seek to hold it to account, even if this was often in a constructive rather than tenaciously critical way. As one interviewee put it, 'you take advantage of being part of the humanitarian [system] but you're also trying to stand outside of the tent and sometimes pee in it'.

Notes

1 However, in 2017, SciDev.Net merged with the Centre for Agriculture and Bioscience International (CABI) and since then has grown its reach and site visits every year. In 2021, its content was seen or heard almost 900 million times, largely due to its radio podcasts, which are disseminated via numerous radio partnerships across Sub-Saharan Africa.

2 Despite their peripheral field position, not all news outlets in our sample suffered from chronic financial insecurity. A handful had more secure sources of funding. For example, Devex is a for-profit, social enterprise that serves as a form of trade magazine for the global development community. It's relatively large journalistic division is cross-subsidised by other, more profitable parts of the organisation, such as its events and careers centre. However, as the only trade magazine in the sector large enough to be able to do this, this model is unlikely to be replicable for other organisations.

Some non-profit news outlets in our sample were under-written by relatively large, multi-year grants, from private Foundations.
3 However, since the end of our period of data collection, there has been some indication that more aid donors are willing to support humanitarian journalists. The New Humanitarian, for example, has recently received funding from the Foreign Ministries of Belgium, Canada, Denmark, Norway, Sweden, Switzerland and the UK. Similarly, since it was established in 2020, HumAngle has received support from the Open Society Initiative for West Africa (OSIWA), the African Transitional Justice Legacy Fund (ATJLF), the Centre for Democracy and Development (CDD) and the MacArthur Foundation.
4 News Deeply's archive of 5,000 issue-driven, articles is now housed by The New Humanitarian in the *Deeply Humanitarian* achieve. Deeply Humanitarian (thenewhumanitarian.org).

References

Benson, R. (2017). Can Foundations Solve the Journalism Crisis? *Journalism Studies.* 11:6. 1–19.

Dominy, G., Goel, R., Larkins, S. and Pring, H. (2011). *Review of Using Aid Funds in the UK to Promote Awareness of Global Poverty.* UK Department for International Development (DFID).

Eyal, G. (2013). Spaces between Fields. In Gorski, P. (Ed.), *Bourdieu and Historical Analysis.* Duke University Press. 158–182.

Fligstein, N. and McAdam, M. (2012). *A Theory of Fields.* Oxford University Press.

Francesca, F. (2014). Secretary General Ban Ki-moon: Save IRIN, a UN-established, award-winning Africa-based news network. Avaaz petition. Posted 27 March 2014. https://secure.avaaz.org/community_petitions/en/Secretary_General_Ban_Kimoon_Save_IRIN_a_UNestablished_award-winning_Africabased_news_network/

Gieryn, T. (1983). Boundary-Work and the Demarcation of Science from Non-Science: Strains and Interests in Professional Ideologies of Scientists. *American Sociological Review.* 48:6. 781–795.

Koehn, D. and Ueng, J. (2010). Is Philanthropy Being Used by Corporate Wrongdoers to Buy Good Will? *Journal of Management and Governance.* 14:1. 1–16.

Medvetz, T. (2012). *Think Tanks in America.* University of Chicago Press.

Orgad, S. (2013). Visualizers of Solidarity: Organizational Politics in Humanitarian and International Development NGOs. *Visual Communication.* 12:3. 295–314.

Örnebring, H. and Karlsson, M. (2022). *Journalistic Autonomy: The Genealogy of a Concept.* University of Missouri.

Örnebring, H., Karlsson, M., Fast, K. and Lindell, J. (2018). The Space of Journalistic Work – A Theoretical Model. *Communication Theory.* 28:4. 403–423.

Schiffrin, A. (2017). *Same Beds, Different Dreams? Charitable Foundations and Newsroom Independence in the Global South.* Centre for International Media Assistance.

Schiffrin, A. (Ed.). (2021). *Media Capture: How Money, Digital Platforms, and Governments Control the News.* Columbia University Press.

Scott, M., Bunce, M. and Wright, K. (2017). Donor Power and the News: The Influence of Foundation Funding on International Journalism. *International Journal of Press/Politics.* 22:2. 163–184.

Scott, M., Bunce, M. and Wright, K. (2019). Foundation Funding and the Boundaries of Journalism. *Journalism Studies.* 20:14. 2034–2052.

Scott, M., Wright, K. and Bunce, M. (2018). *Foundation Support for International Non-Profit News: Mapping the Funding Landscape.* University of East Anglia.

Singer, J. (2015). Out of Bonds: Professional Norms as Boundary Markers. In Carlson, M. and Lewis, S. (Eds.), *Boundaries of Journalism: Professionalism, Practices and Participation.* Routledge. 21–37.

Wright, K., Scott, M. and Bunce, M. (2019). Foundation-Funded Journalism, Philanthrocapitalism and Fraud Allegations. *Journalism Studies.* 20:5. 675–695.

Wright, K., Scott, M. and Bunce, M. (2020). Soft Power, Hard News: How Journalists at State-Funded Transnational Media Legitimize Their Work. *International Journal of Press/Politics.* 25:4. 607.

3 Adding value, amplifying marginalised voices and covering under-reported crises

In the previous chapter, we argued that humanitarian journalists generally suffer from a lack of status, credibility and financial security. We argued that this was a result of their field position – at the 'boundary zone' between the fields of journalism and humanitarianism, which we characterised as a 'space of marginalisation'. But if adopting this peripheral, marginal social space is so challenging, why do they choose to do it? What potential benefits do humanitarian journalists gain from having one foot in both fields? In this chapter, we address these questions by examining the novel professional practices humanitarian journalists were able to engage in as a result of occupying this boundary zone.

The humanitarian journalists in our study all claimed to be able to deviate significantly from dominant journalistic norms and values and instead, adopt their own novel or unique doxic practices. They routinely spoke about having greater 'opportunity', 'openness', 'flexibility' and 'freedom' in their practice. Compared to conventional journalists, they also claimed to be able to, 'be more creative', 'take risks' and 'be [more] experimental'. For example, one editor commented that, 'it is amazing to have the creative room that we have'. Another described her work as 'an opportunity to be a lot nimbler, a lot more experimental and forward-looking'. A third elaborated at length on how this stemmed from a critique of conventional journalistic norms; a perspective shared by many humanitarian journalists.

> I think it is very important that [our] content is not only dictated by 'good journalism'... You [can] become a prisoner of [that] template... I don't want to get straight-jacketed by too much editorial or news value restrictions. I want to free my journalism from that.

DOI: 10.4324/9781003356806-4

This 'freedom' was not always described entirely positively, though. Some interviewees also referred to the professional principles they followed as being 'quite ad hoc' and 'a little bit arbitrary'. One told us, 'I felt myself getting a bit defensive when you asked, 'what is news?'... Defining it is a bit hard and a bit awkward actually... I don't have the luxury of working for a big news organisation that rightly or wrongly thinks it knows what it's doing'. Either way, this apparent flexibility in professional practice appears to support Eyal and Pok's (2011) suggestion that actors occupying the boundary zone between fields operate within an under-regulated 'space of opportunity', where there is less obligation to conform to the doxa of the field. Put simply, humanitarian journalists have a professional freedom to experiment with other ways of performing the job of a 'journalist' and a 'humanitarian'.

The diverse and fluid nature of the practices that emerge from this freedom to experiment inevitably make them difficult to characterise. Despite this, we identify three norms these humanitarian journalists regularly used to distinguish themselves from conventional journalists. Singer (2015:21) refers to these professional norms as 'boundary markers' used, in this case, to perform internal boundary work to distinguish between 'mainstream' and 'humanitarian' journalism. These boundary markers related to news values – in particular, cultural proximity and immediacy – and sourcing practices – including a hierarchy of credibility and humanisation. We show that, in each case, humanitarian journalists rejected these conventional journalistic norms in favour of novel hybrid practices. These included 'reporting under-reported crises', 'adding value' and 'amplifying marginalised voices'.

This supports Eyal's (2013:161) suggestion that the novel practices that actors are able to engage in at the boundary zone between fields are often hybrid combinations of practices and values which 'normally are kept apart', and which can have a 'double meaning' or 'two fold truth'. In this case, we show that 'reporting under-reported crises', 'adding value' and 'amplifying marginalised voices' are hybrid forms of practice that are neither entirely journalistic nor humanitarian but that, 'must be seen as native to the interface between the two' (Eyal and Pok 2011:16). The opportunity to adopt such novel, hybrid practices is a key reason why humanitarian journalists are willing to accept the lack of symbolic and economic capital available at the humanitarian-journalist boundary zone (as discussed in Chapter 2). These novel professional values and practices matter because, alongside other factors such as their target audience, funding models and logistical constraints, they directly shape the content humanitarian journalists produce.

Cultural proximity

The most common 'boundary markers' (Singer 2015) humanitarian journalists used to distinguish themselves from conventional journalists related to news values, or criteria for determining the 'newsworthiness' of events (Galtung and Ruge 1965). Dominant news values within conventional journalism include stories involving elites, celebrity, entertainment, surprise, bad / good news, magnitude, relevance, follow-up and a news organisation's agenda (Harcup and O'Neill 2017). Humanitarian journalists were particularly critical of conventional journalists' adoption of 'cultural proximity' – also referred to as 'meaningfulness' or 'relevance' – as a means of determining which events to cover. Cultural proximity refers to the extent to which the people affected by events are perceived to share a common identity or affinity with the audience. It includes factors such as 'cultural affinity, historical links, geographical distance, economic relations, and psychological or emotional distance' (Joye 2010:256).

Humanitarian journalists argued that the use of cultural proximity, as a news value, in the reporting of humanitarian affairs often produces striking discrepancies between the magnitude, or severity of a crisis and the amount of news coverage it received – just as academic research has repeatedly shown. For example, based on a study of media coverage of six disasters, across 2,000 news articles, from 64 publications, in 9 countries, Franks (2006:281) concludes that, 'there appears to be no link between the scale of a disaster and the media interest it attracts'. Instead, the most consistent predictors of coverage of both foreign disasters and conflicts, across range of studies, are cultural and geographic proximity (Joye 2010; Kwak and An 2014). Cottle (2013) describes the interaction of the news values of magnitude and proximity as producing a 'terrible calculus of death'.

By contrast, humanitarian journalists claimed that considerations of 'cultural proximity' had relatively little influence over their decisions about which stories to cover. As one freelancer explained to us,

> If you're working in Southern Africa and you're trying to sell stories to international outlets, usually they want something that has some direct meaning for their readers, whereas The New Humanitarian would take things that, it matters for those people, [but] it doesn't necessarily have to be connected to the readers.

Almost all the news organisations in our study were international news outlets with a global (largely English-speaking) target audience.

So one reason why they rejected cultural proximity was because there is no one 'culture' among their audience. But this is not the full story. The journalists we spoke to positively embraced humanitarian values, and the desire to see all lives as equal (discussed further, below). This distinguishes them from other, more conventional international news outlets which, despite claims to be 'global', seek stories and frames that have cultural proximity to audiences based in the global North. This was illustrated in our comparative analysis of news coverage of the 2015 Nepal Earthquake by Reuters and TNH. We found that Reuters frequently used terminology that reinforced a traditional domestic-foreign dichotomy, such as 'Westerners', 'foreigners' and 'locals', in order to highlight the relevance of the story to their audience, based primarily in the West. The word 'foreign', for example, was used 32 times in 27 Reuters articles. One such headline read, 'Rescue workers are struggling to recover the bodies of nearly 300 people, including about 110 foreigners… So far, the bodies of nine foreigners have been recovered'. This headline also helps to illustrate that the number of non-Nepalese nationals affected was also repeatedly – in almost every Reuters article – disaggregated from the total numbers of affected individuals. By contrast, TNH never once used either the phrase 'Westerners' or 'foreigners' in any of its 17 reports about the earthquake.

Instead, humanitarian journalists repeatedly claimed their editorial judgements were based, at least partly, on considerations of the extent to which conventional news outlets were (perceived to be) failing to cover a significant issue or event. This was variously referred to as reporting issues that were 'under-reported', 'forgotten', 'untold' or 'neglected' by 'mainstream' news. As one humanitarian journalist explained, 'what we try to do, is to cover underreported stories, neglected emergencies, neglected people, neglected communities'. Another told us that, 'we exist so we can tell the stories that mainstream news outlets aren't chasing – the neglected, forgotten crises in places few reporters go'. (See Chapter 4 for a discussion of the criteria used to determine whether an issue or event qualified as 'under-reported', and Chapter 5 for a discussion of how this compared to other, more conventional news outlets which claim to 'report the under-reported').

Reporting under-reported crises

Not all 'under-reported' issues were considered newsworthy, however. One humanitarian journalist told us that '[being] under-reported in itself isn't a sufficient criterion for us tackling a subject. The story itself needs to fall into our world'. In other words, it needs to fit the subject area, or beat, of the news outlet – whether global health, global development, or humanitarian affairs (see Chapter 4). Similarly, in the quotation below, the reference to a story needing to be 'really important' as well as 'under-reported', helps to highlight that severity or 'magnitude' remained an important news value for humanitarian journalists, even if 'cultural proximity' was not.

> The thing I like a lot about being at News Deeply is... that we can really give space for stories that are really important but there aren't a lot of news outlets out there that are going to be interested in covering them. That is one thing I found really exciting. I really like getting the story pitches from freelancers because all these story ideas that people have had simmering for a long time but they can't find anybody to take them, it is like it is perfect for us; that is exactly what we are looking for.

On occasion, this focus on reporting under-reported, rather than culturally proximate, events led humanitarian journalists to appear to provide an 'early warning', particularly for emerging or slow-onset crises. This is because they may have been covering events long before they were reported by conventional news outlets. In this respect, several interviewees were keen to highlight instances where their coverage had preceded a rapid escalation in mainstream reporting, as in the case below. Other examples mentioned included the Rohingya refugee crisis and the crises in Yemen and the Central African Republic.

> Often we'd do a story that... turned out to be a big thing. But we did it so early... it wasn't connected as a news break... We were covering Boko Haram years before [mainstream international news].

This emphasis on reporting under-reported crises is informed, at least partly, by the humanitarian principle of moral equivalence, or the idea that the provision of humanitarian assistance must be based on need alone, rather than nationality, race, religion, caste, age, or gender (Barnett 2011). This principle of human equivalence was frequently evoked by humanitarian journalists when discussing their news values. For example, one respondent told us that,

> We think that people suffering is equal and deserving of respect and response.... We believe suffering is equal wherever and

equally deserving of attention and response... All the attention here and no attention there... is continually motivating to try to redress that imbalance.

Similarly, in an open letter to their readers, TNH's managing editor wrote,

Our proposition is based on the following beliefs: Human suffering – no matter where it takes place – is equally deserving of attention, understanding and relief. People on opposite sides of the planet are not so different: we all want to be safe, to put our kids into school, to live a decent life.

From this perspective, to decide to report on one crisis over another, based on a consideration of cultural proximity, or the perceived cultural affinity of your audience with those suffering, would be to discriminate based on nationality, race and/or religion. Instead, according to the humanitarian principle of moral equivalence, the severity and urgency of 'need' should be the determining factor when prioritising assistance. As one interviewee explained, 'it becomes news when significant numbers of people are suffering'.

However, humanitarian journalists did not always interpret 'need' in entirely the same way as humanitarians – who define it purely in terms of the severity of human suffering. As the above quotations illustrate, humanitarian journalists often placed an additional emphasis on the extent to which an issue or crisis *needed attention*. In doing so, they drew on the journalistic notion of 'bearing witness', or the moral imperative to acknowledge other people's suffering by communicating their traumatic experiences to the wider world in ways that attempt to change the witnessed reality (Frosh and Pinchevski 2009; Tait 2011; Pantti 2019). Such 'changes' could include reassuring victims that they have not been forgotten, generating empathy, resisting acts of denial, or preventing the recurrence of such suffering (Pantti 2019). As Zion, Briskman and Loff (2012:73) put it, witnessing 'acts as testimony from which [political] action can begin'. Another humanitarian journalist drew on this concept of 'bearing witness' more explicitly, arguing,

I look at humanitarian crises as being where people need the public eye, and the players involved in it to be held to account, the most. For me, it is the underreported issues... as well as identifying where people are most in need of the public eye to be watching.

Following this interpretation, humanitarian journalists often perceived themselves as serving both a humanitarian and a journalistic function through their practice because, by reporting on severe and under-reported instances of human suffering, they could help to address their 'need' (for attention). This is made clear in the following interview extract,

> Would I think what I'm doing is a humanitarian service by highlighting something? In a way, yes… If there is drought in Southern Africa, in Zimbabwe, we would be highlighting it because we think it's an important story. Are we doing that as a humanitarian service to the world? Yeah, probably. You're saying, 'Look here, this is an important story, people are ignoring it, it's got to be highlighted. About a third of Zimbabwe is going hungry'.

Given this interpretation of 'reporting under-reported crises' – as relating to considerations of both moral equivalence and a need for attention – we regard this as a hybrid humanitarian-journalistic value, just as Eyal and Pok (2011) suggest. One interviewee even made this connection themselves, saying, 'for me, the tie between news and humanitarianism is very clear… I always felt that my job as a journalist is to tell stories that are not being told'.

In summary, when considering what issues or events to cover, humanitarian journalists generally rejected considerations of cultural proximity in favour of covering seemingly under-reported instances of severe human suffering. As a result, they were reporting on the armed conflict in the Donbas region of Ukraine in 2021, for example, when it was almost completely ignored by most other news outlets, and when global media attention did switch to covering Ukraine in 2022, humanitarian journalists gave it comparatively less attention – focusing instead on 'forgotten crises' elsewhere in the world. This important practice stems partly from the interests of their target audiences, but also from an adherence to the humanitarian principles of moral equivalence, and a journalistic concern for bearing witness. This hybrid humanitarian-journalistic practice is one way that humanitarian journalists take advantage of the under-regulated 'space of opportunity' that exists at the 'thick boundary zone' between the fields of humanitarianism and journalism (Eyal 2013).

Immediacy

Another common 'boundary marker' humanitarian journalists used to distinguish themselves from what they described as 'mainstream' journalism was 'timeliness', or an evaluation of the immediacy of events. Consideration of the extent to which events are 'new', or have happened recently, is central to conventional conceptualisations of journalism (Harcup and O'Neill 2017). However, our interviewees claimed to be far less concerned with immediacy. They variously described themselves as producing, 'certainly not heart-breaking news', or 'super-quick, reactive content', as not having a 'hard-newsy mainstream focus' and as not working for 'a hard news organisation'. For example, one editor said, 'what we do is explanatory journalism around global affairs issues, including humanitarianism. We don't break a lot of news'. Another interviewee said, 'we don't try to cover any blow-by-blow events... it takes longer here... We don't have to churn stories out. Which is nice, although there's a lot to be said for the adrenalin of that in the newsroom'.

The relative lack of concern for 'timeliness' amongst humanitarian journalists was also revealed in both of our comparative analyses of news coverage. For instance, 67% of all Reuters articles about the 2015 Nepal earthquake referred to an incident or other 'news hook' which took place in the previous 24 hours, compared to only one TNH news story (6%). Similarly, Table 3.1 shows that TNH had by far the lowest proportion of 'breaking news'[1] (9%) in its coverage of South Sudan and Yemen in 2017, out of any of the nine news outlets in our sample.

It is important to highlight that humanitarian journalists did retain a degree of concern for immediacy. Their coverage was not entirely off-agenda or disconnected from the news cycle. As one respondent told us,

> We're not a hard news organisation, but you know, we're reactive to what's going on... I mean, something big might happen, for

Table 3.1 Percentage of news items about South Sudan and Yemen in 2017 in the form of 'breaking news'

	South Sudan (%)	*Yemen (%)*
BBC World Service	94	80
CGTN (Africa and Americas)	31	40
The Guardian	21	26
CNN International	20	33
Al Jazeera English	17	43
Devex	13	50
The Washington Post	10	42
Mail Online	0	40
The New Humanitarian	0	17

example, a major disaster like an earthquake and within a day we might have a take on it, or a live piece. So [we're] in tune with the news agenda.

There were also some exceptions to this general trend. One humanitarian journalist described their news outlet as, 'trying to be a place where, we are not going to break a ton of stories, but [we are] having more immediate newsiness than often second-day type stories'. Similarly, one Devex journalist explained that 'there has actually been a fair bit of breaking news with things to do with the Trump administration, but, as a general rule, there is not that much'. In their coverage of the conflicts in Yemen and South Sudan, on average, 25% of Devex's news items took the form of 'breaking news' – more than TNH (9%), for example, but still considerably less than BBC World Service (87%).

Humanitarian journalists gave several reasons to explain their relative lack of concern for immediacy. This included the challenges of working with stringers in locations with poor internet connections and the time taken to reach sources in different time zones. Several also suggested that 'breaking news is not that big a thing' within the subject area they covered, since humanitarian assistance involves a lot of slow onset emergencies, or 'really difficult, long-burning crises, like in DRC and northern Uganda, where it is the same story day in, day out'. For some humanitarian journalists, their target audience was a determining factor in enabling them not to rely so heavily on timeliness as a news value. For instance, one Devex journalist told us that, 'for an audience of experts and people who are going to be continuously interested in the subject, there is a willingness to engage with the story that isn't necessarily tied to a breaking news event, as opposed to trying to just draw general interest audience'. This suggestion is supported by the results of our survey of aid workers, which found that they judged 'breaking news' to be the least valuable aspect of news about humanitarian affairs. As shown in Figure 3.1, only 31% of respondents chose it as one of their 'top three' most important aspects of such news. Instead, the most valuable aspects were expert analysis (58%), investigative reporting (54%) and consistent coverage of ongoing crises (52%).

In addition to these various practical or logistical considerations, many humanitarian journalists also felt strongly that being governed by a concern for immediacy led to coverage that was 'repeating', 'copying', 'replicating' or 'very similar' to the outputs of most other news organisations. This perspective was well articulated by one editor who told us,

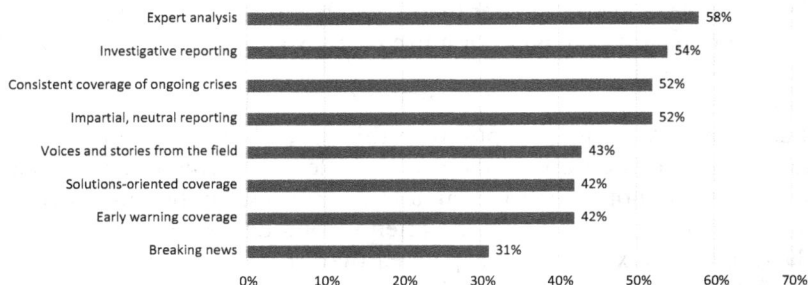

Figure 3.1 Aid workers' perceptions of the most important aspects of news coverage of humanitarian issues and crises in 2018 (Percentages reflect the proportion of respondents selecting each issue within their 'top three') (n=1626).

My normal reaction when anyone pitched a story [was] I would do a Google News search and say, 'well yeah, but you know, forty-five people wrote about this last week. What are we adding?'... There's no point in doing another version of the same thing everyone else is talking about. Unless you can add a new take to it, what's the point?

Another interviewee referred to this as 'regurgitated' coverage, while another described this as a tendency to report on something, 'just for the sake of it'.

Adding value

As a result, humanitarian journalists' professional practice was shaped, far less by a concern for immediacy, than by an ambition to 'add value' to existing coverage. Indeed, 'adding value' was one of the most used phrases amongst our respondents when discussing news values. Interviewees referenced the same idea when they spoke of 'looking for a gap' or 'holes' in existing coverage, 'second-day stories', 'companion stories', 'add[ing] an additional slice', 'looking for unusual angles' and bringing 'fresh life' or 'fresh perspectives' to a story. As one respondent explained, 'looking at what has already been done or what hasn't been done, is the goal... Coming up with other angles to add to the conversation in a way that hasn't been done yet'. The following quotation was typical of the way interviewees compared conventional journalistic practices to this practice of 'adding value' by supplementing an existing news story.

> [When working] for Voice of America, I felt like my objective each day was to identify whatever the most pressing information was for my audience, and just get it out there as quickly as I possibly could, but in a way that was objective, fair and balanced, meeting all the standards of journalism. Now... my goal is really to introduce something new to a conversation that is already taking place.

But whilst there may have been a clear consensus amongst humanitarian journalists about the importance of 'adding value' over 'timeliness', there was far less agreement about how to achieve this. In general, they sought to 'add value' in their reporting by providing, in some way, further context, analysis or explanation to an event or issue that they thought mainstream news coverage was not providing. This was variously referred to as providing, 'in-depth content', a 'deeper story', 'deeper background', 'additional analysis' or an 'analytical perspective'. Interviewees also spoke of covering, 'the context behind crises', 'putting the shades of grey into things' and providing 'more sophisticated, nuanced, complex reporting'. In practice, this involved a range of approaches such as providing further details about the complex causes or underlying 'systemic drivers' of an issue or event, or discussing the various financial, political and security implications of a change in policy. For example, one editor encouraged their staff to, 'juxtapose, debunk, turn upside-down, look ahead, look back, dig, question, expose, unpack, muse'.

In explaining this approach to 'adding value', humanitarian journalists often contrasted their coverage with the 'superficial' or 'simplified' coverage provided by more timely, 'hard' news. For example, one interviewee explained how she felt their coverage of the 2015 European refugee crisis differed to most other news organisations.

> A lot of news outlets, following that disaster in the Mediterranean, were quite superficial. It was about, 'all these people are coming, what are we going to do'? Just reporting what politicians were saying, basically, all very much from the European perspective. Whereas I think the *Guardian* and hopefully what we were trying to do, was look deeper at; why are people coming in the first place? Where are they coming from? Why are they coming from there? Which routes are they using? What's facilitating that? What's making it so unsafe?... We were always very good at making clear

that there is a deep complexity to a lot of these conflicts in Africa, just as there are in other places, but that isn't always picked up perhaps by other media. I think just being utterly committed to trying to explain the complexity of situation.

This general focus on explanatory journalism was also reflected in the ways interviewees characterised the format of their outputs – as 'features', 'analyses', 'briefings', 'explainer pieces' and 'long-form' coverage (rather than 'daily news' or 'short news briefs'). However, in characterising their professional practice in this way, humanitarian journalists were also careful not to jeopardise their professional identity as 'journalists'; arguing that such analytical coverage still qualified as (a 'different kind' of) journalism. To do so, several interviewees contrasted their practice with that of an 'analyst'.

Putting together an analytical report is completely different than, you know, journalism… I don't want to become an analyst, because that's a different job… If we went in the direction of more analysis than journalism, and I wasn't really able to focus on journalism, that's a situation in which I wouldn't see myself remaining here.

This focus on providing longer-form, explanatory journalism helps to explain why coverage produced by specialist news outlets was, generally, relatively long. For example, Table 3.2 shows that the average word length of online news articles about South Sudan and Yemen in The New Humanitarian (1,459 words) and Devex (994 words) were significantly longer than the other news outlets in our sample, including

Table 3.2 Average word length of news items about South Sudan and Yemen in 2017 for eight different international news outlets

	South Sudan	Yemen	Overall Average
The New Humanitarian	1,415	1,502	1,459
Devex	920	1,068	994
Washington Post	1,003	684	844
Guardian	994	737	831
Mail Online	962	675	819
Al Jazeera English	799	496	648
CNN International	526	679	603
CGTN (Africa and Americas)	268	288	556

the Washington Post (844 words), the Guardian (831 words) and the Mail Online (821 words).

Maintaining a degree of concern for timeliness, as a news value, was also important for retaining the professional identity of a journalist because it enabled them to 'show that we have our finger on the pulse', as one respondent put it. However, during our interviews, several humanitarian journalists also argued that immediacy and 'adding value' (by providing original context or analysis) can be mutually exclusive. They were only able to 'take the extra time' required to research and produce longer-form, explanatory journalism *because* a more relaxed approach to the importance of timeliness 'alleviated the time pressures' in their job.

Different formats, different approaches

Another, less common, way of 'adding value' was for humanitarian journalists to experiment with different formats, platforms and 'ways of telling a story' in order to increase the appeal or 'accessibility' of coverage of an issue. As one interviewee explained,

> It doesn't have to be a 1,500-word analysis to add value. We can express that information in different ways that may in fact have more value for different types of readers. We've done a lot of interactive maps, interactive timelines, we've played around with cartoons, we've played around with infographics.

For some humanitarian journalists – particularly those working for Devex, News Deeply and BRIGHT Magazine – 'adding value' was achieved by adopting a solutions-oriented approach to their reporting, or by focusing on responses to social issues as well as the problems themselves (see McIntyre 2019). As one journalist explained,

> We are not a breaking news site, so if a famine is declared in South Sudan, we are not going to write a story that says, 'Famine has been declared in South Sudan'. But we would dive into that subject and look at what makes this famine unique compared to historic famines in the region or approaches to addressing the famine that have not been tried before that are innovative. That is, I think, what sets us apart.

Interestingly, though, our survey of aid workers found that they did not value solutions-oriented journalism as highly as many journalists assumed. Figure 3.1 shows that fewer respondents selected 'solutions journalism' as one of their 'top three' most important aspects of news about humanitarian affairs, than most other aspects (42%).

This focus on 'adding value', especially within non-profit news outlets, is perhaps unsurprising as it is increasingly championed as key to the future of journalism, particularly within discourse relating to the 'crisis of journalism'. Perhaps the most famous proponent of this view is Jeff Jarvis (2014:5) who argues that 'the key question journalists must ask today is how they add value to the flow of information in a community, a flow that can now occur without mediators – that is, without the media'. Specifically, Jarvis (2014:4–12) suggests that 'building a stronger relationship with their audiences' will enable journalists to 'add greater value to a community's knowledge' and that this will be the 'foundation for a new business strategy for the news industry'. Within this perspective, then, the main purpose of 'adding value' is 'to find sustainable – that is, profitable – support for news' via audiences (Jarvis 2014:5). 'Adding value', Jarvis (2014) suggests, can be achieved not just by creating original content but also by curating existing content, convening conversations, incubating ideas, organising events and advocating certain causes.

There was certainly evidence to suggest that some humanitarian journalists adopted this particular understanding of 'added value'. Two journalists even explicitly cited the work of Jarvis (2014) when discussing the term. For example, one told us that,

> We've been reading Jeff Jarvis's book – *Geeks Bearing Gifts* – and he talks about news, now more than ever, needing to be a service, so you're providing information that is a service to people and if we're looking at business models, that's the only way they're going to pay for it.

However, this was not the most common interpretation of the term. Indeed, the concept of 'added value' is not just a feature of the journalistic field. As discussed in Chapter 1, it is also a key feature of the humanitarian field, where it is used to emphasise the principle of 'making the most difference' (Krause 2014). When most humanitarian journalists used the phrase 'added value' they appeared to be referring to the concept of 'making the most difference to people's lives', which derives from the field of humanitarianism, rather than journalism. In other words, they were trying to 'do good' rather than develop the business case for their journalism. In the following interview extract, for example, the humanitarian journalist associates 'added value' with 'being useful,' rather than 'competing with other outlets'.

JOURNALIST: I think, looking at what has already been done or what hasn't been done, is the goal.

INTERVIEWER: So is it about differentiation? It's about trying to find the thing that hasn't been done. Is that coming from a place of wanting to compete with other outlets?

JOURNALIST: It is just to add value to the conversation. We want to be useful.

Similarly, in the following quotation, another humanitarian journalist highlights 'long-term impact' and 'moving the conversation ahead' as key to their focus on 'added value'.

We are not just into news that is reactionary. We are more into covering stuff and writing about the issues that will have more of a long-term impact... Also to combine those on-the-ground stories with something that moves the conversation a little ahead beyond just reporting these stories.

In Eyal's (2013) terms, humanitarian journalists' emphasis on 'adding value', rather than 'timeliness', is a product of a hybrid combination of norms and values, with a 'double meaning' or 'two fold truth', made possible by the 'space of opportunity' at the humanitarian-journalism field boundary.

Humanisation and a hierarchy of credibility

Humanitarian journalists also distinguish themselves from 'mainstream' journalists in the way they used sources. Specifically, they rejected the common practices associated with a 'hierarchy of credibility' and 'humanisation'. In their place, they favoured 'amplifying marginalised voices'.

A 'hierarchy of credibility' refers to the inclination within conventional journalism to ascribe more credibility to official or elite sources, such as government spokespeople or those from international institutions – than to non-elite sources, such as representatives of trade unions, local business, or ordinary citizens (Lawson 2021). It is an important 'strategic ritual' (Tuchman 1972) within conventional journalism because citing seemingly authoritative sources helps reporters maintain a sense of objectivity by appearing to remove their presence or opinion from a story. However, when applied to coverage of humanitarian affairs, a 'hierarchy of credibility' was frequently criticised by humanitarian journalists for helping to marginalise the voices and experiences of affected populations in favour of the agendas of official or elite sources. As one interviewee told us,

> I did a lot of coverage of Syria, and... there is so much coverage on the conflict, on the players in that game. Not that there isn't a need for that. Absolutely there is. But sometimes I think there is a severe lack of telling of the voices [of those affected] who need to be heard.

Humanitarian journalists were particularly critical of what they saw as conventional journalists' tendency to rely on press releases from official sources. One respondent described this as the 'danger of giving undue attention to the press releases, the spokespeople, and the David Millibands'. He went on to say that,

> On a personal basis, I would much prefer to reflect upon grass-roots, more than an NGO, or in the field, where possible... I try to give more of a voice to the people who are the recipients of humanitarian relief or aid... to try to actually focus on those voices, rather than the voices of those who are in charge.

It was in this context that almost all humanitarian journalists spoke of their desire to amplify marginalised voices through their reporting, or to include a range of direct quotations, usually from affected actors. As one interviewee explained, 'the reason why I do humanitarian news, and I am sure the reason why other people do it, is because we are giving voice to the voiceless. With news in general, I don't see that happening at all'. Another commented that,

> We always made sure that our sources are actually the people affected, if at all possible. If you can go there and talk to the people and get their voices in the story, that, for me, was always the ideal. We had this maybe romantic notion of being the voice of the voiceless and trying to give a voice to people who were actually affected; to weave in the story, instead of speaking for them.

According to our interviewees, this focus on 'amplifying marginalised voices' differs in subtle but important ways from the mainstream practice of using sources to 'humanise' a story. The latter refers to a tendency to cite affected citizens, particularly as the opening or 'lead' for a news item – and is especially common in news coverage of humanitarian crises (Cottle 2013; Ardèvol-Abreu 2016). Indeed, many of the journalists working for international broadcasters who we interviewed as part of our wider study discussed how they implement this practice. For example, one such journalist told us that they had,

A commitment to telling authentic, real stories and hearing those stories from real people as it's happening to them... That commitment to the authenticity of experience and capturing it and not managing it too much, not mediating it too much... We're all striving for the authentic, eyewitness, 'What happened to you? Tell me the story. Show me your life.' It wouldn't be unfair to say it's a piece of stock reporting to go to the feeding station, to go to the local field hospitals. You could always guarantee a few shots with that.

The references in this quotation, to 'not managing' or 'mediating' eyewitness testimonies 'too much' highlight the related concern amongst conventional journalists that, when identifying affected citizens to interview, 'you're not being filtered through an NGO who is looking for a particularly shocking angle, for example'. As one Guardian journalist told us, 'we always want to hear from people on the ground, not through the NGOs'.

The frequent use of 'humanisation' as a sourcing practice within conventional news coverage of humanitarian affairs stems from two influences. First, it derives from a general predisposition to seek out 'human interest' material in an effort to 'personalize the news, dramatize or "emotionalize" the news, in order to capture and retain audience interest' (Semetko and Valkenburg 2000:96). For example, in the following quotation, an editor at the BBC World Service suggests that including the voices of affected citizens has an 'intrinsic editorial value' because it signals that they are 'close to the story'.

Ultimately, a lot of these stories are best told through those who are living them and experiencing them. Actually, I think that also demonstrates that we're close to the story, because the more experts and people you're piling in from London and Washington and everything else suggests you're doing the story from a distance... I think that, in a way, there's intrinsic editorial value in that.

Second, the sourcing practice of 'humanisation' stems from what Cottle (2013:233) describes as the well documented tendency within conventional journalism to, 'purposefully craft and inscribe their news reports with a thinly veiled but transparent "injunction to care"', when reporting on disasters. Cottle (2013:244) argues that an 'injunction to care' is, 'enacted through crafted narratives designed to engage, humanize, "sense-ize" and "bring home" the plight of distant others – strangers still – but people not so unlike ourselves and deserving of our recognition and care'. Indeed, the conventional journalists we interviewed often spoke of, 'trying to package a product to try and get people to care', 'encourag[ing] people to have empathy for other people who are less fortunate' and 'bringing some sense of compassion to a story'.

Conventional journalists' focus on 'humanisation' and a 'hierarchy of credibility' within their sourcing practices is further illustrated in Figure 3.2. This graph shows the extent to which different sources were quoted, within international news coverage, on a range of different UK bulletins, in 2016 (see Magee and Scott 2016). It highlights, firstly, that the dominant voices in almost every news bulletin were 'local citizens' – making up between 31% and 42% of all sources. This appears to reflect a strong concern for 'humanisation'. Secondly, it shows that expert sources and local government sources were also extremely common in such news coverage – reflecting a similarly strong concern for a 'hierarchy of credibility'. It also shows a distinct lack of use of NGOs as sources – by any news bulletin. Overall, local and international NGOs made up just 2.5% of all sources.

Third, and perhaps most striking, is that Figure 3.2 reveals a remarkable level of consistency in these apparent sourcing practices, across a wide range of very different news outlets. This illustrates that both sourcing conventions are a widespread feature of conventional

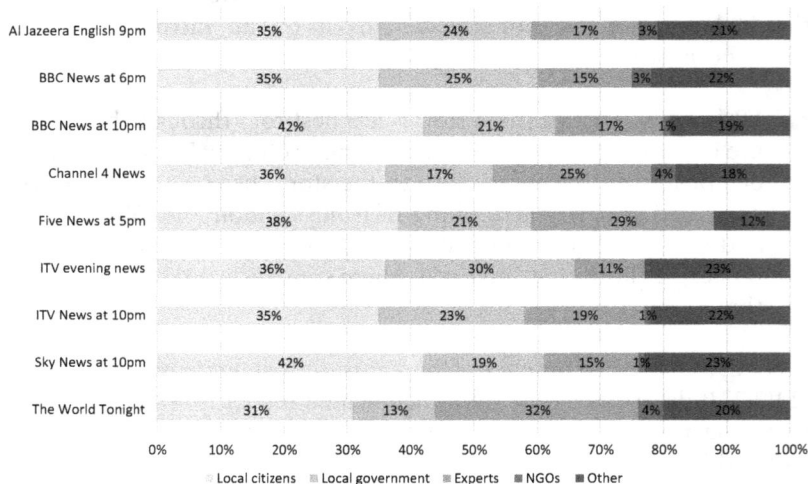

Figure 3.2 Who speaks in international news, within different UK news bulletins, in 2016.

journalistic practice. Indeed, when presented with these findings, none of the seven editors of these bulletins that we interviewed considered them either surprising or especially troubling. One described these results as stemming from a 'formula' in the way international stories are told. Cooper (cited in Magee and Scott 2016:8) has referred to this as 'template reporting' whereby – 'you get the vox pops, then the local government, then the expert to say "this is how it works"'.

Amplifying marginalised voices

In sharp contrast, when discussing their ambition to 'amplify marginalised voices', humanitarian journalists did not emphasise their desire to cite affected individuals to 'get people to care' or to 'capture audience interest'. Instead, they emphasised, once again, the humanitarian principle of moral equivalence. Specifically, they said their sourcing practices were driven by a concern for 'addressing an imbalance in whose voices are heard' or bringing 'more equality of attention'. As one humanitarian journalist explained,

> The one thing I do want to do is continue to tell that person's or that family's story because they have a right to be heard as much as a billionaire has a right to be heard for his or her investment story or project they are doing half way around the world. This person's voice matters. It might be two million people affected, but here is one person, one family that does have a voice and, hopefully, should be heard or will be heard.

Furthermore, for these humanitarian journalists, 'amplifying marginalised voices' could be achieved, not only by including more direct quotations from affected citizens, but by including the voices of other affected actors who might also be perceived as marginalised. For example, one interviewee described 'affected people' as including, not just citizens, but also 'rebels... government officials... [and] think-tanks'. Another also referred to 'community and diaspora organizations... [and] emerging aid actors in the Gulf' as 'un-consulted parts of the humanitarian architecture'. Put simply, for humanitarian journalists, affected citizens were not the only potential marginalised actors. Given this, they tended to cite a relatively wide range of a-typical and often local sources. For example, Table 3.3 shows that, in their coverage of South Sudan and Yemen, Devex was the most likely news outlets in our sample to quote representatives of local and international businesses (5%), while TNH was most likely to cite international experts (12%).

Table 3.3 Sources used by different news organisations in their coverage of South Sudan and Yemen in 2017

	Local/Affected Citizen (%)	Multilateral Organisation (%)	Local Government/Authority (%)	Local NGO (%)	International NGO (%)	International Expert (%)	Business (%)	Other (%)
Al Jazeera English	20	25	11	1	12	6	0	24
BBC World Service	29	21	24	0	12	0	0	15
CGTN (Africa and Americas)	14	24	19	3	4	3	0	34
CNN International	17	30	9	2	15	2	2	21
Daily Mail	24	14	29	0	24	0	0	10
Devex	2	33	7	0	30	10	5	15
Guardian	14	26	7	3	21	6	1	23
The New Humanitarian	10	24	4	4	20	12	0	27
Washington Post	13	24	7	0	18	10	0	28

This focus on marginalised actors in general, rather than only affected citizens, also led some humanitarian news outlets to focus on the voices of aid workers. This is also reflected in the result of our content analyses. For example, in its coverage of the 2015 Nepal Earthquake, TNH was significantly more likely to cite representatives of international NGOs (22%) and local NGOs (8%), compared to Reuters (8%/0%). Similarly, Table 3.3 shows that in their coverage of South Sudan and Yemen, Devex and TNH were the news outlets most likely to quote representatives of international NGOs and local NGOs respectively. Interestingly, they were also the least likely to cite affected individuals (2% and 10%). In fact, several interviewees argued that there were circumstances where it would be preferable to include the voices of aid workers rather than affected citizens. For example, one humanitarian journalist told us that, if they were reporting on UK government aid, 'I would much, much rather be able to reflect the views and opinions of different workers in the field, and hear them speak candidly about how they feel about the department and about what it does'. Similarly, in the following quotation, a humanitarian journalist working for a news outlet whose target audience includes professionals working in humanitarian policy and management explains the value of speaking, not only to refugees, but to, 'the people who ran… a refugee camp'.

> Do you remember 'the jungle' in Calais? That refugee camp that got knocked down? That is obviously a huge story in Europe, [and] certainly fits within the humanitarian and development context. Every media organisation in the world has covered the jungle at some stage and everybody goes in and finds the Eritrean refugee and they talk to him, and, quite rightly, are moved by his story, and they tell his story to the world, and that's great. It's a story of great journeys across Africa and risk taking, and you wind up in Calais and you get treated horribly and you are trying to make it to Britain. That is a fantastic story. [But] it is not a Devex story at all. We sent a crew there to do a story, and I watched the video, and there is not a single refugee being spoken to in that video. What they did, which is exactly what they should do, is they went and spoke to the people who ran the camp. The camp was existing in this weird non-official space because it wasn't officially set up by the [French] government. So it wasn't subject to all these rules and regulations that it desperately needed to be. It was a really interesting question of, practically speaking, how on earth do you run a camp in these circumstances? That became the story, and that is actually of real interest to our audience because they can

go, 'Oh, that's how that works. We don't do that.' So that is how we covered the jungle, and no one else had done that story because everyone else is talking to the refugees with their powerful stories, which is exactly what their audience want because their audience is mainstream. But ours isn't.

This extract highlights, once again, the crucial role that the target audience of a news outlet plays in helping to determine the journalistic norms and values that news producers can adopt.

One final trend within the sourcing practices of humanitarian journalists was a deliberate intention, especially by female news producers, to include more voices of women and girls in their coverage. For example, one interviewee who 'quit a stable staff job' in order to 'do foreign news', told us,

I am always drawn to stories about women and children… because we know that those voices are not heard enough or depicted properly in the media. I thought I could do that with a level of empathy, whilst holding people to account… I care about trying to accurately and fairly depict what women's experiences are, and their voices, in my coverage, because I don't think there is enough of it. But when there is a lot of coverage about these issues, especially looking at gender-based violence or femicide around the world, it is treated like a movie plot line.

In summary, humanitarian journalists' sourcing practices were governed, not by the conventional journalistic norms of 'hierarchy of influences' and 'humanisation', but by a concern for 'amplifying marginalised voices'. This practice was informed by the humanitarian principle of moral equivalence, or a desire to 'address an imbalance in whose voices are heard' (rather than to offer an 'injunction to care') – leading to both a diversity and a relative freedom in humanitarian journalists' sourcing practices. It even led some humanitarian journalists to favour NGOs representatives, as sources, over affected citizens. Given this degree of freedom, and the influence of a humanitarian principle, this represents another example of the kinds of creative, hybrid professional practices that humanitarian journalist can engage in at the humanitarian-journalism field boundary. It also further supports Eyal and Pok's (2011:18) suggestion that this boundary zone operates as a 'space of opportunity' where, 'the rules about what one can legitimately do/combine are relaxed'.

Conclusion

In this chapter, we have shown that humanitarian journalists have a relative freedom in determining their professional norms and values. This freedom is at least partly a reflection of the field position they adopt – at the 'thick boundary zone' between the fields of humanitarianism and journalism, which Eyal (2013) characterises as a 'space of opportunity'. Humanitarian journalists use this freedom to deviate from dominant journalistic norms and values – especially 'cultural proximity', 'immediacy', 'hierarchy of credibility' and 'humanisation'. Instead, they adopt their own, novel professional practices, including reporting under-reported crises, adding value through explanatory or solutions-oriented journalism and amplifying marginalised voices. These practices are also shaped by their target audience, funding models and logistical considerations. We have also shown that Eyal (2013) is right to suggest that the novel practices actors engage in at the space-between-fields are often hybrid combinations of practices and values. In this case, humanitarian journalists' practices often stem from hybrid journalistic-humanitarian values.

Note

1 In our study, a news item was considered 'breaking news' if the principal 'news hook', or event on which the story focused, occurred within 24 hours of the article being published.

References

Ardèvol-Abreu, A. (2016). The Framing of Humanitarian Crises in the Spanish Media: An Inductive Approach. *Revista Española de Investigaciones Sociológicas.* 155. 37–54.

Barnett, M. (2011). *Empire of Humanity: A History of Humanitarianism.* Cornell University Press.

Cottle, S. (2013). Journalists Witnessing Disaster: From the Calculus of Death to the Injunction to Care. *Journalism Studies.* 14:2. 232–248.

Eyal, G. (2013). Spaces between Fields. In Gorski, P. (Ed.), *Bourdieu and Historical Analysis.* Duke University Press. 158–182.

Eyal, G. and Pok, G. (2011). From a Sociology of Professions to a Sociology of Expertise. *Expert Determination Electronic Law Journal.* 1–28. http://exp ertdeterminationelectroniclawjournal.com/eyal-g-and-pok-g-2013-from-a-sociology-of-professions-to-a-sociology-of-expertise/

Franks, S. (2006). The CARMA Report on Western Media Coverage of Humanitarian Disasters. *The Political Quarterly.* 77:2. 281–284.

Frosh, P. and Pinchevski, A. (Eds.). (2009). *Media Witnessing: Testimony in the Age of Mass Communication*. Palgrave Macmillan.

Galtung, J. and Ruge, M. (1965). The Structure of Foreign News: The Presentation of the Congo, Cuba and Cyprus Crises in Four Norwegian Newspapers. *Journal of Peace Research*. 2:1. 64–90.

Harcup, T. and O'Neill, D. (2017). What Is News? *Journalism Studies*. 18:12. 1470–1488.

Jarvis, J. (2014). *Geeks Bearing Gifts: Imagining New Futures for News*. CUNY Journalism Press.

Joye, S. (2010). News Media and the (De)construction of Risk: How Flemish Newspapers Select and Cover International Disasters. *Catalan Journal of Communication and Cultural Studies*. 2:2. 253–266.

Krause, M. (2014). *The Good Project: Humanitarian Relief NGOs and the Fragmentation of Reason*. University of Chicago Press.

Kwak, H. and An, J. (2014). *Understanding News Geography and Major Determinants of Global News Coverage of Disasters*. Computation and Journalism Symposium '14, New York.

Lawson, B. T. (2021). Hiding Behind Databases, Institutions and Actors: How Journalists Use Statistics in Reporting Humanitarian Crises. *Journalism Practice*.

Magee, H. and Scott, M. (2016). *Small Screen. Big World: The International Content of the UK News*. International Broadcasting Trust (IBT).

McIntyre, K. (2019). Solutions Journalism: The Effects of Including Solution Information in News Stories About Social Problems. *Journalism Practice*, 13:8.1029–1033.

Pantti, M. K. (2019). Journalism and Witnessing. In Wahl-Jorgensen, K. and Hanitzsch, T. (Eds.), *The Handbook of Journalism Studies*. *ICA Handbook Series*. Routledge. 151–164.

Semetko, H. and Valkenburg, P. M. (2000). Framing European Politics Acontent Analysis of Press and Television News. *Journal of Communication*. 50:2. 93–109.

Singer, J. (2015). Out of Bonds: Professional Norms as Boundary Markers. In Carlson, M. and Lewis, S. (Eds.), *Boundaries of Journalism: Professionalism, Practices and Participation*. Routledge. 21–37.

Tait, S. (2011). Bearing witness, journalism and moral responsibility. *Media, Culture & Society* 33:8, 1220–1235.

Tuchman, G. (1972). Objectivity as Strategic Ritual: An Examination of Newsmen's Notions of Objectivity. *The American Journal of Sociology*. 77. 660–79.

Zion, D., Briskman, L. and Loff, B. (2012). Psychiatric Ethics and a Politics of Compassion: The Case of Detained Asylum Seekers in Australia. *Bioethical Inquiry*. 9:1. 67–75.

4 Fifty shades of humanitarianism

Our central argument in this book is that humanitarian journalists have unusual but important professional values and practices due, in part, to their position at the 'boundary zone' between the fields of journalism and humanitarianism. We have already established, in Chapter 3, that some of these practices stem from deviations from conventional *journalistic* norms. But what of their understandings of 'humanitarianism' and how this affects their practice?

'Humanitarianism' – just like 'journalism' – is a deeply contested concept. The philosophies, principles and goals of humanitarianism vary internationally and have shifted over time in relation to changing geopolitical contexts (Barnett 2011). For these reasons, humanitarianism has been described as both a 'contested terrain' and something of a 'sticky signifier, capable of holding on simultaneously to multiple discourses and meanings' (Cottle and Cooper 2019:2). Within the West, for instance, there are longstanding tensions between the 'chemical' strand of humanitarianism, which seeks only to provide immediate relief to those who are suffering; and the 'alchemical' strand, which also tries to prevent suffering by challenging its structural causes of suffering (Barnett 2011; Orgad 2013).

The distinctions between humanitarian action and related concepts such as human rights and global development are also inherently blurred. Most humanitarian crises around the world are protracted, with UN humanitarian appeals lasting, on average, for seven years (Valente and Lasker 2015). Humanitarian emergencies can, therefore, no longer be viewed as entirely reactive and 'short-term' because they often overlap with the longer-term structural and complex socio-economic processes commonly associated with global development (OCHA 2022).

In this chapter, we review how the humanitarian journalists in our study understand the contested concept of 'humanitarianism'. We find

DOI: 10.4324/9781003356806-5

that while there was some agreement amongst interviewees about several key underlying features of this term, in general, their understandings of this concept were relatively broad and inconsistent. This is well illustrated by the following interview extract in which a humanitarian journalist identifies 'scale' and a need for 'intervention' as core elements of humanitarian action, but which also reveals the ambiguity in their understanding. We characterise this as the adoption of an 'ambiguous-humanitarianism', in contrast what Tester (2010) has described as alternative 'common sense' and 'professional' understandings of humanitarianism.

INTERVIEWER: Can you define for me what you think humanitarianism is?

JOURNALIST: [Laughs] God that's hard, actually! It's trying to alleviate suffering, especially in the context of a crisis that's caused by a conflict, disaster or some kind of large-scale event and it's trying to intervene with some kind of response to alleviate that, whether it's international or local. It's pretty broad isn't it?

INTERVIEWER: Where are the limits of humanitarianism?

JOURNALIST: I think it's always going to be a discussion and it always has been, since I've been working here.

We go on to argue that such conceptual 'fuzziness' (Eyal 2013) is not simply the result of humanitarian journalists' individual habitus, or dispositions. It is, once again, shaped by their field position. Specifically, it is, as Eyal (2013) argues, necessary for ensuring that the boundary zone they occupy remains a 'space of opportunity', where they can produce their own novel, hybrid professional practices, which we described in Chapter 3. Put simply, maintaining a degree of conceptual fuzziness gives humanitarian journalists greater freedom to report what they want, how they want. This matters because it enables them to cover a wider range of issues related to extreme human suffering, to provide the broader, political context to such crises and to reflect the perspective of a wide range of actors – whilst still retaining the professional identity of 'humanitarians'.

An ambiguous humanitarianism

All humanitarian journalists demonstrated an awareness of at least some key principles of the concept of 'humanitarianism' and of what differentiates it from related concepts, such as human rights and global development. In the following quotation, for example, a distinction is

made between humanitarianism and human rights based on the scale
or magnitude of human suffering involved – although there is also an
acknowledgement that this distinction is 'blurred'.

> Human rights abuses – where they are on a large scale – can be
> a cause or a result of humanitarian crises and so will often fall
> within our remit. But one individual human rights abuse is not a
> humanitarian issue. There's a lot of blurriness there, but I think
> the core is clear.

Indeed, the scale of human suffering was perhaps the most common
way in which humanitarianism was distinguished from related concepts. As another interviewee explained, 'once it reaches a certain
threshold of crisis – in terms of effect on a number of people – then we
cover it'.

Some interviewees had a more subtle understanding of the significance of scale, though, suggesting that humanitarianism referred to
the need for *international* intervention or situations where the scale of
a crisis exceeded the capacity of the local community to respond. One
humanitarian journalist described it in the following way; 'I'd say, and
it's debated fiercely of course, that a humanitarian crisis is a situation
so bad it requires intervention or could potentially lead to an intervention'. However, respondents were also generally careful not to simply
equate humanitarian action with the activities of organisations working within the international humanitarian community. For instance,
one interviewee described the humanitarian sector as,

> A tiny part of any response. I don't care if it's in Somalia or in the
> Congo – most of the work is not done by those people. Most of the
> work is done by ordinary Congolese, it's done by Diaspora, it's
> done by the private sector, it's done by all these people.

Surprisingly, very few interviewees adopted a purely 'chemical' strand
of humanitarianism or sought to be non-political. Instead, most took
the view, as expressed in one news outlets' editorial guidelines, that, in
a country experiencing a humanitarian crisis, a detailed examination
of politics is 'even more legitimate... [since] humanitarian situations
often have political causes'.

Aside from scale, the other key distinguishing feature of humanitarianism, especially compared to global development, concerned time,
or the apparent urgency or immediacy of events. As one interviewee
put it, 'I guess the distinction is that development work is long-term

aid and humanitarianism is more short-term. I think that's generally accepted. To me, though, I think they need to work more together. I think there should not be as much of a distinction'. This emphasis on immediacy was also implied by the frequent use of the term 'emergencies' to refer to the particular subject matter of a humanitarian news 'beat'.

Despite identifying some of the conventional 'fault lines' (Barnett and Weiss 2011:8) between humanitarian action and other, related concepts, there was also a strong tendency to minimise or play down these differences – as each of the quotations above suggests. This was achieved in several ways. Those working for news outlets with an exclusive focus on covering humanitarian affairs repeatedly emphasised the 'interlinked', 'interlocked', 'interconnected' and 'blurred' relationship between humanitarianism and global development. Specifically, they would frequently highlight the idea that, 'a failure to address certain development issues could… lead to a humanitarian crisis' or that a humanitarian crisis 'is, by definition, rooted in what came before, will have consequences afterwards and will have a political dimension'. This 'blurred' relationship, they suggested, made it 'difficult' – if not 'ridiculous' or even 'nonsensical' – to 'separate humanitarian issues from development issues'. The proposed solution, therefore, was to adopt what several described as a 'holistic' approach to reporting humanitarian affairs, whereby a relatively wide range of issues could legitimately be covered as long as there was some 'link' or 'fig-leaf' to, broadly defined, 'humanitarian' concerns.

Humanitarian journalists working for news outlets with an explicit focus on global development regularly took a similar stance, suggesting that humanitarian action and development issues 'go hand in hand' or are 'meshed together'. For example, one respondent asked, 'what is the line between humanitarianism and development? I don't think anyone knows anymore?' Another told us, 'I don't see them as totally isolated and I don't see clear-cut boundaries or walls between them… I guess I would bunch them all together'. However, there was also a tendency within these more development-focused news outlets for some individuals to describe humanitarian affairs as a 'subset' or 'small part of' global development. As one respondent explained, 'we cover development very broadly. So, within my job, humanitarian stories are a subset of what we cover'. In either case, journalists working for these development-focused news outlets were in general very relaxed about covering stories closely linked to humanitarian affairs.

Finally, some humanitarian journalists, working for a range of different outlets, minimised the differences between humanitarianism and related concepts by defining it as a 'cross-cutting' or 'over-arching' category, or as an 'umbrella term' or 'broad brush label'. For example, one respondent said, 'I would suggest that journalism that looks at development issues, journalism that looks at human rights, journalism that looks at security, it all, to me, falls in that humanitarian basket, really'. Another told us,

> Our main areas of focus are global security, global development, human rights, climate change and global women's issues, including reproductive health issues... I think humanitarian[ism] is cross-cutting throughout many of them. There is no reason not to have a [separate] humanitarianism category. But it is, in my mind, cross-cutting a lot of these issues.

In summary, while our interviewees did demonstrate an awareness of some key principles of the concept of humanitarianism and of what differentiates it from related concepts, these differences were minimised. By minimising these differences, our respondents ultimately ended up adopting relatively vague and inconsistent definitions of humanitarianism. Most were fully aware of this, describing their approach to covering humanitarian issues as, 'not always logical', 'quite ad hoc', 'debatable', 'fuzzy', 'confused' and even 'arbitrary'.

A degree of inconsistency within understandings of humanitarianism is to be expected, given that the concept is deeply contested. What was surprising, however, was the *degree* of inconsistency and ambiguity within understandings of humanitarianism – both between journalists working within the same news outlets and even within individuals own personal accounts. For example, the following interview extract reveals how, in the course of one interview, a journalist working for a news outlet with an explicit focus on reporting humanitarian affairs gave a number of very different definitions of humanitarianism and ultimately concluded that they were 'very confused' about the concept. Such inconsistencies and levels of uncertainty were not uncommon within interviewees' testimonies.

INTERVIEWER: If I was to say to you, 'what is humanitarianism'? Where would you start?

JOURNALIST: I think I would think of it in a very straightforward sort of United Nations, agency-based, NGO support [way], bringing those human issues to light; seeing news through that human lens. I haven't really thought about it, actually... I'm trying to get my head around the beat of [human] trafficking and, to me, it almost

felt that this whole crisis of exploitation and trafficking is a result of hyper capitalism itself... I think there is something in there
about that economic violence. Having worked on so many of those
stories, especially in a place like India, I think that is a humanitarian concern.

INTERVIEWER: That is really interesting... You started off by talking
about humanitarianism as being to do with the UN agencies, the
aid agencies, disasters and crises, and you have now moved into
another area, which you describe as being characterised by concerns about economic exploitation. I wonder if I could just take
you back to the term of humanitarianism, then. What does that
mean about how you define or see humanitarianism, if it includes
economic exploitation?

JOURNALIST: Now I am suddenly feeling very confused about what I
think humanitarianism is.

There were also significant differences between accounts of
humanitarianism given by journalists working within the same
news outlets. One interviewee told us that there had 'always been'
an 'ongoing debate' about understandings of humanitarianism
within their news organisation. Another said that they, 'tend to
agonise over what is humanitarian reporting... [but] don't really
have the answer yet'. For example, when reporting on the issue of
female genital mutilation, another interviewee admitted they 'had
been very inconsistent on it. Sometimes we've called it a humanitarian issue, and sometimes it's a development issue and I'm not
sure we've worked out what our position is on that'.

Overall, given the level of inconsistency and ambiguity within their
understandings of humanitarianism, and their tendency to minimise
differences with related concepts, most of our respondents accepted
that they 'take a fairly broad view of what constitutes 'humanitarian''.

Alternative understandings of humanitarianism

To get a clearer picture of how humanitarian journalists understood
the concept of humanitarianism, it is useful to compare their testimonies with those of other journalists we spoke to, as part of our wider
study. This included journalists who used to work for Alertnet – a
'humanitarian news portal', established in 1997 by the Reuters Foundation, which described itself as 'the world's leading independent humanitarian news service covering natural disasters, conflicts, refugees,
hunger, diseases and the human impacts of climate change'. In 2008,

AlertNet was consolidated into News.Trust.org, the Thomson Reuters Foundation's main news service. Journalists working for AlertNet operated with what one interviewee described as 'a strict definition of "humanitarian" to guide us on whether we would report on a crisis or not. Why would we cover a particular earthquake in Nepal, say, but not one of equal size in California?'. In particular, one of the 'key questions' they considered 'was whether the disaster overwhelmed the local capacity to cope or respond'.

AlertNet's approach corresponds with what Tester (2010:7) characterises as 'the humanitarianism of the professional humanitarians'. This refers to an adherence to dominant humanitarian principles of independence and moral equivalence, as well as the notion of political neutrality – but also the parameters of professional debates related to these principles (Tester 2010). As such, this definition does not correspond with either the 'chemical' or 'alchemical' strand of humanitarianism, or any other any other form of distinction amongst professional humanitarians. Rather, it encompasses them. As Tester (2010:7) explains,

> Think of a kaleidoscope. If it is looked at one way, it is a collection of shattered moving pieces that occasionally come together into coherent patterns but spend a lot of time in a somewhat confused condition. This is how the commentators on humanitarianism tend to see the matter. They are committed to a coherent principle and to the action that follows from it, and yet they know that as soon as the tube is looked down, all that is likely to be seen is a chaos of overlapping parts, gaps, color clashes, and incoherence. They see crisis. Yet there is another way of looking at a kaleidoscope. Yes, all of the pieces are in a mess, but the circumference of the tube contains them and they often come together into coherent patterns, even though the coherence can and does disappear very quickly. From this way of looking, the kaleido-scope is taken for granted and is largely invested with trust, and quite how it all works is significantly less important than the fact it sometimes does. The kaleidoscope might not be looked at terribly often, but when it is, it shows what is looked for.

The only individual we spoke to who defined humanitarianism in this way was a former AlertNet journalist. When asked what 'humanitarian' means, they responded,

> It clearly relates to the core humanitarian principles, which are embedded in the origins of a humanitarian movement, which is

that humanitarian aid should be – and I would apply this to humanitarian information as well – delivered on the basis of need, not on the basis of expediency or anything else. So it is apolitical; it is neutral... So there is a neutral need to help people because they need help, whoever they may be, whatever their religion or whatever their political status or the geopolitical concerns.

It is worth noting, though, that those individuals and news outlets with a stronger orientation towards the humanitarian field generally offered more precise and consistent definitions – mirroring more closely what Tester (2010:7) terms, 'the humanitarianism of the professional humanitarians'. For example, individuals working for news outlets whose target audience consisted primarily of professionals working in the aid sector (rather than more general, less specialised, audiences) were more likely to make clear distinctions between humanitarian and development coverage, as in the following quotation.

What is the difference in reporting for the development audience versus the humanitarian audience? They are just totally different people in different worlds. Both can run to similar kinds of content. Both need a place for practical advice. But it would be different. A lifestyle piece for a development professional might be something that would be more field-based and long term, as opposed to a humanitarian piece, which is like, 'OK, you have to deploy in six hours, what do you pack?' That is the difference in useful content... We are sensitive to the fact that people who work in humanitarian aid have different needs and have a different work environment than a lot of people who work in international development... I think everyone here is just very sensitive to that, because all of our reporters... have a vested interest or background in that.

As this interviewee suggests, individuals with previous experience of working in the aid sector were also more inclined to operate with a clearer distinction between humanitarian and development coverage – especially compared to those with a stronger journalistic background. For example, one interviewee, who had worked in the development sector, suggested that some of their journalistic colleagues, 'didn't really understand what the word 'humanitarian' means, and they confuse it with human rights'.

But while few humanitarian journalists in our study fully adopted 'the humanitarianism of the professional humanitarians', there were also limits to the breadth of their definitions. This can be illustrated most effectively by comparing them to the much more broad and vague understandings of humanitarianism adopted by non-specialist journalists, working for more generalist or conventional news organisations, such as the BBC World Service, CNN, the New York Times and Sky News. When asked about 'humanitarianism', these journalists draw largely on what Tester (2010:6) refers to as 'common sense humanitarianism' or 'the humanitarianism of the inexpert humanitarians'. As Tester (2010:7) explains,

> For most people most of the time humanitarianism is... not something thought about terribly much. It is just there, like the sports results, celebrity gossip, and television listings. Humanitarianism has become a naturalized component part of the ordinary Western cultural and moral milieu... What is common-sense humanitarianism? It is the humanitarianism of media audiences who rely on unquestioned myths to make sense of the suffering of others.

Expressed more formally, common-sense humanitarianism refers to the self-evident, uncritical, personal and moral obligation to help suffering others, emerging from sensate emotional desires such as sympathy or compassion (Tester 2010). For example, a senior journalist working for an international broadcaster explained that, 'being a humanitarianist is to act and believe in that way that helps one another and helps other humans'. Another non-specialist journalist told us that humanitarianism, 'means doing good to humans. Promoting something good for them'.

According to Tester (2010:24), one of the key 'unquestioned myths' underpinning common-sense humanitarianism is the idea of 'human community', which 'assumes a fundamental unity in all humans throughout the world'. Non-specialist journalists frequently evoked this idea when they defined humanitarianism in terms of 'the effect of events on human beings', as in the following quotation.

> Humanitarian news, for me, is the kind of news which focuses on the human race as a whole, and the conditions in which they are living and the problems they are facing, their suffering, and highlighting that... Basically, telling people stories that involve human bits.

Similarly, in the following quotation, a non-specialist journalist equates humanitarian news with stories about 'real people'.

INTERVIEWER: Would you describe any of your outputs as humanitarian?

JOURNALIST: I don't know. What do you mean by 'humanitarian'? There's a commitment to telling authentic, real stories and hearing those stories from real people as it's happening to them. I don't know whether that's humanitarian. I think that's very human and very real… that commitment to the authenticity of experience and capturing it and not managing it too much, not mediating it too much… What we've definitely done is not just shooting [the Syrian] war, but a huge range of the experiences of what that war is doing to real people… So we do have a commitment to showing the, if you want to call it, humanitarian side of it, and not just be on the front line, looking out to the latest incoming shell.

Finally, non-specialist journalists appealed to 'common-sense humanitarianism' when they equated humanitarianism with 'human interest' stories. The sentiments expressed in the following quotation were common amongst such news producers.

Humanitarianism, I think, is about, human interest… Humanitarian reporting is all about, just telling the human interest stories, telling the stories of the basic needs of the people, the basic things that affect the real people… Humanitarian stories, human stories, stories that affect the people directly, stories that people live every day, be it drought, be it social economic issues that people face, be it issues of inflation, cost of living, conflict, and things like that. That, to me, is humanitarian reporting. Just telling the story of the real people and the issues that affect them.

These non-specialist journalists also regularly failed to distinguish between humanitarianism and related concepts. In fact, they gave little indication that they were even aware of some of its basic underlying principles. In the following quotation, for example, the terms 'humanitarian' and 'human rights' are used interchangeably.

INTERVIEWER: How much of the work that you do is focused on humanitarian crises?

JOURNALIST: In this part of the world, a lot… We did a fair bit on people who have been convicted of Lèse-majesté [the insulting of a monarch].

INTERVIEWER: Would you give that as an example of a humanitarian crisis?

JOURNALIST: Yes, human rights. Yes, humanitarian issues. And also, in Vietnam, dissidents who get imprisoned or who get harassed, I see that as a humanitarian / human rights category.

However, not every non-specialist journalist adopted the perspective of 'common-sense humanitarianism'. Some defined humanitarianism as referring specifically to the activities of international institutions that explicitly describe themselves as 'humanitarian' – including INGOs and some UN agencies. This institutional definition of humanitarianism is evident in the following quotation.

> For me, when you say humanitarian, I think of the NGO world – humanitarian agencies, humanitarian networks, [the] humanitarian industry… I am thinking of NGOs and white knights coming out in expensive Toyota land cruisers to save the day.

The contrast between understandings of humanitarianism within specialist and non-specialist news outlets and was particularly clear in the testimonies of respondents who moved from the later to the former. One such journalist explained that, 'once you've been there for a certain period of time, you understand the remit much better, so you stop thinking 'we should be covering that story'. You think, 'Oh, that's not a [humanitarian] story'. Another stated that, 'you learn what [the editor] wants, eventually, but it's not straightforward'.

In summary, understandings of humanitarianism adopted by humanitarian journalists were not as vague as the common-sense understandings held by most non-specialist journalists. Neither were they as specific, detailed, or consistent as, 'the humanitarianism of the professional humanitarians' (Tester 2010). Instead, they fell somewhat in between; adopting the humanitarianism of ambiguous humanitarians.

Strategic ambiguity

Eyal (2013:177) argues that the kind of conceptual ambiguity described here is a necessary requirement for a 'space of opportunity' between fields to exist because, without it, actors would not be able to 'exploit the fact that it is an under-regulated space', to produce their own novel practices. In short, 'ambiguity is itself an asset' (Eyal and Pok 2011:18).

The idea that ambiguous understandings of 'humanitarianism' served a strategic purpose for our interviewees was made clear on several occasions when interviewees explicitly related their 'freedom' to experiment with news values with their 'struggles' over the definition of humanitarianism. For example, in the following quotation, the 'freedom' to deviate from a conventional news agenda is directly equated with a seemingly perpetual uncertainty over the nature of their news beat.

> What is the point of news where there's 1,200 stories on the same thing? *What is the point?* It's bonkers... These things seem very inefficient to us... We enjoy the freedom of not marching to that band but it puts us in the uncomfortable position of having to figure out what our beat *is* and that's what we're doing on Slack[1] every day.

Similarly, in the following quotation, a respondent explains that 'stretching the rules' of what constitutes humanitarianism and 'adopting a very liberal attitude' towards it, enables them to do 'more interesting stories'.

> We struggle hard with our definition of humanitarianism versus development, but for me... it's whatever affects lives and livelihoods... [and] anything that affects stability. I mean this is on the outer extremes, to allow us to do some of the more interesting stories that people would otherwise deem political... I have a very liberal attitude to what is humanitarianism... I'll stretch the rules if it's a really, really good story about something that affects ordinary people.

There is also a specific suggestion here that avoiding characterising humanitarianism in terms of a commitment to neutrality enables humanitarian journalists to cover issues that might otherwise be 'deemed political' such as human rights abuses.

Importantly, this ambiguous approach to humanitarianism also gave journalists a strategic advantage: it enabled them to seek funding from a wider range of sources. As our previous research has shown, non-profit funding sources, particularly philanthropists and private foundations, are key to the production and sustainability of humanitarian journalism. Some funders prioritise particular audiences, subjects or approaches to journalism in their grant calls, or partnership formation (Scott, Bunce and Wright 2019). Thus, taking a flexible approach to the definition of humanitarianism can enable these organisations to frame their work in a way that makes it relevant to a much wider range of funders. They can, for example, apply for funding to report on topics related to development or human rights.

By contrast, for journalists covering humanitarian affairs for more general news outlets, there is no such strategic benefit to departing from a common sense understanding of humanitarianism, which most of their audience shares, and adopting a somewhat narrower definition. Put another way, there is little benefit in orienting themselves towards the humanitarian field because they gain and validate their existing capital entirely from the journalistic field, by adhering to conventional journalistic norms and values. This is made clear in the following quotation from a former non-specialist journalist who describes himself as thinking 'in traditional journalistic terms'.

INTERVIEWER: Where does humanitarianism end and where does human rights or development begin?
JOURNALIST: It is not something I have thought about in terms of those labels. I have just been thinking more in traditional journalistic terms of telling a good story and an interesting story and an informative and enlightening and entertaining story.

Their role, as conventional journalists, is to determine whether events are newsworthy or not, according to conventional news values, and to cover those events as they would any other. Given this, the only occasion in which the concept of 'humanitarianism' may be useful to non-specialist journalists is in helping to define a specific 'beat' or thematic area of focus – just as the terms 'business', 'environment' and 'education' are used to define other news beats. This explains why some non-specialist journalists equated humanitarianism with the actions of the international humanitarian community. For most non-specialist journalists, though, the concept of 'humanitarianism' was generally seen as irrelevant or, 'not a useful label' for describing or informing any aspect of their work.

Conclusion

In conclusion, the humanitarian journalists we interviewed generally adopted a relatively broad and inconsistent understanding of humanitarianism. Our aim in highlighting this adoption of an 'ambiguous-humanitarianism' is not to suggest that humanitarian journalists are wrong to do so. Rather, it is to demonstrate that this ambiguity is strategically useful because, if these journalists were to define humanitarianism more precisely and consistently, or adopt 'the humanitarianism of the professional humanitarians', this would restrict their 'creative room' to experiment with journalistic practices. At the same time, though, their desire to draw (selectively) on humanitarian values to produce novel, hybrid practices still required them to adopt a stronger orientation towards the humanitarian field than most other journalists – preventing them from adopting a 'common sense' approach to defining humanitarianism.

Note

1 Slack is a popular online collaborative software that supports remote journalists to work together, share and develop story ideas. Our previous research has shown that it can be a very important space for the development of norms, values and organisational culture within a news organisation – including, for example, where journalists deliberate on the definition and boundaries of humanitarianism (Bunce, Wright and Scott 2018).

References

Barnett, M. (2011). *Empire of Humanity: A History of Humanitarianism*. Cornell University Press.

Barnett, M. and Weiss, T. (2011). *Humanitarianism Contested: Where Angels Fear to Tread*. Routledge.

Cottle, S. and Cooper, G. (Eds.). (2019). *Humanitarianism, Communications and Change*. Peter Lang.

Bunce, M., Wright, K., and Scott, M. (2018). 'Our newsroom in the cloud': Slack, virtual newsrooms and journalistic practice. *New Media & Society*, 20:9, 3381–3399.

Eyal, G. (2013). Spaces between Fields. In Gorski, P. (Ed.), *Bourdieu and Historical Analysis*. Duke University Press. 158–182.

Eyal, G. and Pok, G. (2011). From a Sociology of Professions to a Sociology of Expertise. *Expert Determination Electronic Law Journal*. http://exp ertdeterminationelectroniclawjournal.com/eyal-g-and-pok-g-2013-from-a-sociology-of-professions-to-a-sociology-of-expertise/

OCHA. (2022). *Global Humanitarian Overview 2022*. United Nations Office for the Coordination of Humanitarian Affairs.

Orgad, S. (2013). Visualizers of Solidarity: Organizational Politics in Humanitarian and International Development NGOs. *Visual Communication*. 12:3. 295–314.

Scott, M., Bunce, M., and Wright, K. (2019). Foundation Funding and the Boundaries of Journalism. *Journalism Studies*. 20:14. 2034–2052.

Tester, K. (2010). *Humanitarianism and Modern Culture*. Penn State University Press.

Valente, R. and Lasker, R. (2015). *An End in Sight: Multi-Year Planning to Meet and Reduce Humanitarian Needs in Protracted Crises*. United Nations Office for the Coordination of Humanitarian Affairs.

5 Is humanitarian journalism a field-in-the-making?

The final step in our ambition to better understand the professional norms and practices of humanitarian journalists is ask – to what extent they occupy their own unique field, or at least a 'field-in-the-making' (Eyal and Pok 2011:17)? Addressing this question is important because it will enable us to better understand how to support this form of practice. Answering this question also allows us to highlight further key features of humanitarian journalists' professional practices, including their willingness to collaborate, awareness of each other, target audiences and professional identities.

We have already presented some evidence to suggest that humanitarian journalists may, to some extent, occupy their own unique field. In Chapter 3, we argued that, despite a relative freedom to experiment with novel professional practices, humanitarian journalists share several common practices, including 'reporting under-reported crises', 'adding value' and 'amplifying marginalised voices'. We also established, in Chapter 4, that they share similar, ambiguous understandings of 'humanitarianism', which allow them to maintain these practices and which set them apart from actors positioned more firmly within the journalist and humanitarian fields.

However, as we discussed in Chapter 2, establishing a shared community of practice – or field – requires more than a relatively common set of doxic values and a shared conceptual ambiguity (Fligstein and McAdam 2012). Other key field-defining features include symbolic differentiation, field-specific symbolic capital and field-building (Krause 2014). Therefore, in this chapter, we ask (1) if and how these actors differentiate themselves from each other (symbolic differentiation), (2) whether they seek the same kind of status and prestige (symbolic capital) and (3) the extent to which they or others seek to professionalise and institutionalise this area of expertise (field-building). In doing so, we also compare humanitarian journalists' norms and values

DOI: 10.4324/9781003356806–6

with those operating in within Al Jazeera English and the Thomson Reuters Foundation, and consider the influence of the journalistic intermediaries, such as the Pulitzer Centre on Crisis Reporting and One World Media. We ultimately conclude that, since they lack almost any form of institutionalisation, humanitarian journalists are currently best understood as operating at a 'boundary zone' (Eyal 2013), rather than a field.

Collaborating rather than competing

Perhaps the most striking aspect of the relationship between humanitarian journalists was that many were not even aware of each other and could not name many, or in some cases, any, of the other specialist news outlets in our study. For example, after describing some of these news organisations to one interviewee, they commented, 'I'm actually not familiar with most of the ones you mentioned'. Similarly, when asked to name other news outlets they compared themselves to or thought were similar, many respondents claimed that their journalism was 'unique'. One respondent told us that, 'it is hard to compare [with other news outlets] because we do feel really unique', while another said that 'there is not another outlet that I see.... doing something similar'.

Interviewees who were aware of other news outlets within our study generally did not describe themselves as competing with them. For example, one editor told us,

> I don't see The New Humanitarian as a rival... I think they are great, but I don't see them as a competitor at all. We don't really have one... Our premise was that people weren't doing these stories... [so] there's no one to compete with.

The following quotation from another respondent is particularly revealing because it not only suggests, once again, the relative lack of a competitive motivation, but also that this represents a change in professional practice from when they were 'working in general news'.

> I don't think we perceive ourselves as being in competition with Devex. We are not trying to be first before them. We wouldn't necessarily pop open champagne corks to celebrate if we have what we would see as an exclusive and Devex do not. If I had any residual sense of competition, it is what I carry over from working in general news.

Indeed, several other respondents explicitly compared their current experiences with the competitive nature of conventional journalism. One interviewee told us that, 'journalists agonise about things that no one else gives a toss about, right? I mean, the energy that the tabloids spend on exclusives. We just don't give a flying whatever about whether they've got the only story'. Another explained that, 'we don't enjoy the kind of competition which gets journalists up in the morning'.

Alongside this lack of competition amongst humanitarian journalists was an absence of a 'hierarchy of worth' (Eyal 2013:176), which characterises most fields. Since they were not in competition, it was not possible or necessary to establish which news outlets were 'better' or more prestigious.

Rather than characterising their relationship with each other in terms of competition, our respondents referred to 'partnerships' or, most commonly, to 'collaborations'. For instance, a senior editor told us, 'I don't like to think too much in terms of competition because I think we're all in the same team'. Another interviewee explained that these relationships were 'not competitive, it is more collaborative. We don't chase stories to break news, so we don't have that kind of competitive relationship with people'. However, such collaborations were largely aspirational. Although several interviews spoke of an ambition to 'share information... [and] tip offs', a general lack of time and resources meant that such initiatives were often not realised.

This contrasted with the perspective of almost every conventional journalist we spoke to, within our wider study. These interviewees readily described themselves as having a 'competitive motivation' vis-à-vis other news outlets. For example, an editor at the BBC told us that,

> Obviously, we pay attention to what ITV News, Channel 4 News, Sky News, and others are doing. The competition is strong, and that's healthy. Of course, if they've got a scoop or [if we] feel like they've delved into something in a more effective way than we have, then that gives us pause for thought.

This was also the case for journalists working for news outlets that positioned themselves as 'correctives' to mainstream journalistic practice, which often claimed to adopt similar practices to humanitarian journalists, such as Al Jazeera English and the Thomson Reuters Foundation. These respondents said, as previous studies have shown, that the news outlets they worked for differentiated themselves from others primarily as part of a strategic positioning within a competitive journalistic field (Benson and Neveu 2005). For example, one such interviewee described Al Jazeera English as 'deliberately different' from BBC World and CNN to fill 'a gap in the market'.

> We have to forge our different place in the market. So we're trying to give people an alternative that's different to what's there at the moment... It is about differentiating. It is about looking for something others have not done.

Another interviewee linked this competitive motivation directly to their coverage of humanitarian affairs, arguing that they, 'started to allocate a lot of resources to humanitarian stories because we wanted to take the lead and we wanted to set the news agenda'.

This competitive motivation was also linked directly to other journalistic practices. For example, several interviewees described Al Jazeera English's focus on reporting 'under-reported' stories as linked to a pursuit of exclusivity, claiming that, 'they want a story that is underreported so that they can own it'. Similarly, another interviewee described Al Jazeera English's ambition to be a 'voice of the voiceless' as being partly, a 'way of saying that [this] is a platform to tell stories that a brand like CNN won't'. Another described 'bringing the context to the story' as a key way to 'distinguish ourselves from others, especially Sky News and Fox News'. By contrast, we argued in Chapter 4 that humanitarian journalists focus on reporting under-reported crises, adding value and amplifying marginalised voices. This stems from a hybrid combination of journalistic and humanitarian values that meet in the 'space of opportunity' provided by the boundary zone – rather than from a competitive motivation within the journalistic field.

However, it is important to note that a general lack of competition amongst humanitarian journalists does not, by itself, indicate that this social space is un-fielded. Graves and Konieczna (2015) argue that collaborative elements of newswork may also be a symptom of a broader realignment of the journalistic field. Similarly, Marchetti (2005) points out that many specialised journalistic subfields lack a strong sense of competition or differentiation. Transnational investigative journalism, for example, requires intense cross-border collaboration between news outlets but remains firmly within the journalistic field (see Heft 2021) and has even been described as contributing to 'field repair' (Graves and Konieczna 2015).

There were also some exceptions to this general lack of symbolic differentiation amongst humanitarian journalists. As in the following quotation, several interviewees defined their practice, not just by comparing themselves with what they termed 'mainstream' journalists (as discussed in Chapter 2) but by differentiating themselves from each other.

> I think each outlet does things better than the other outlets. For example, The New Humanitarian is really great at the insider stuff from the UN agencies and some really nice in-depth stories [whereas] Devex does the donor stuff really well. I would say we are talking to the [same] people who are reading Global Development on The Guardian... Telling the human side of the story.

In making these comparisons with other specialist news outlets, several interviewees even referred directly to a distinct community of news organisations. For example, one interviewee said they, 'see an ecosystem of news outlets in this arena, but no direct competitors'. Although this might indicate that the social space occupied by humanitarian journalism is not entirely un-fielded, this quotation also reminds us of its general lack field-like properties, such as symbolic differentiation. Indeed, another interviewee described this social space as a 'field that no one thinks is a field', acknowledging that while there are some actors that report on similar topics, few saw it as a 'field'.

Playing different games

The key reason why humanitarian journalists did not see themselves as competing was that they were each seeking different symbolic and economic resources. This lack of 'common stakes' is revealed in several ways. First, when respondents did compare themselves, the most common area of differentiation was their target audiences. For example, one journalist had plotted the perceived position of their news outlet in relation to other, similar organisations on a graph where the x-axis indicated the degree of complexity and the y-axis reflected the degree of specialism of their target audience. The importance of news outlets' target audiences, as a point of comparison, is also highlighted in the following quotations.

> Obviously, we are not Devex, because Devex has its own audience. We also don't have the reach of Goats and Soda NPR. But we are definitely getting a better audience share of people inside the industry than, say, NPR. So we are closer to them than Devex, but not all the way that far for the general audience.
>
> There's a difference in audience, I think. DAWNS Digest was created specifically as news clips service for people who are

professionals in the global development and humanitarian field…. Our audience is a little different. It is a little more focused on Americans, in particular, but also… a lot of the posts are framed in a way that make them a little more shareable than just a straight news clips service.

These different target audiences reflect the pursuit of different sources of economic and symbolic capital derived from either humanitarian or journalistic authority, as discussed in Chapter 2. Put another way: humanitarian news outlets were not competing for the same things.

Second, there was little evidence to suggest that humanitarian journalists sought the same forms of status or prestige, or that there was a unique form of field-specific symbolic capital they were competing for (Fligstein and McAdam 2012). Perhaps the strongest indication of this was that our respondents did not even share a common phrase or terminology to refer to the social space they collectively occupied or to their common professional practices. Very few interviewees voluntarily used the term 'humanitarian journalist' themselves and no other term, such as 'crisis reporting', was used by more than one individual. On occasion, when introducing our research, we used the phrase 'humanitarian journalism' ourselves, to characterise our area of interest. While some interviewees adopted this phrase themselves in the subsequent conversation, a number also explicitly rejected it. For example, one interviewee told us,

I never got into it labelling what I do as 'humanitarian journalism'. I just wanted to flag that up. What I do is try to tell stories of people and trying to get people to care about the country and the situation, which, obviously, inevitably, brings us round to the fact that there are human beings involved in every aspect and sector. So, yes, I felt like I never really got into it to be a humanitarian journalist.

Similarly, although we argued in Chapter 3 that humanitarian journalists did share some common practices, such as 'reporting underreported crises' and 'amplifying marginalised voices', these shared norms were identified and named primarily by us, within our analysis, rather than by participants themselves. Put differently, while respondents often agreed that they were reporting on similar issues or topics, they generally did not see their styles of reporting as similar. In short, our respondents generally saw little value in marking themselves out as 'humanitarian journalists'.

Third, our respondents emphasised the challenges of communicating the value of their professional practices to others. For example, several interviewees reflected on how they found humanitarian issues a 'harder sell' or 'not really sexy', compared with coverage of other international issues. One respondent told us that, 'the bar of a story about those issues [is] even higher, as far as getting a project approved and getting our partners engaged' because it's not likely to be perceived as 'the next big thing'. Similarly, in the following quotation, an editor reflected on how their perceived lack of profile may be partly the result of the complexity of what they are trying to achieve.

> We're not noticed nearly as much as we should be and that comes [partly] from… what we're trying to do. It doesn't resonate with people because it's not in a simple sexy tagline, or because it's just got too many layers. Taking something that is, if you want to explain it in a nuanced way, quite complex, and whittling it down to a simple message that can make people feel something, is a challenge.

In a rare exception, one journalist told us that covering humanitarian affairs, 'is your chance to show that you care about human beings through covering the stories others are not covering'. This statement suggests that this individual does see unique symbolic value in the specific practice of reporting under-reported crises – because it enables you to 'show that you care'. In this respect, it appears to combine the humanitarian value of 'moral equivalence' with the journalistic values of 'novelty' and 'exclusivity'. Adding emphasis to the symbolic value of this practice, this individual went on to argue that it, 'made a name for Qatar, and made Al Jazeera famous, which made people think 'why is a government in Qatar supporting such a Freedom of Speech project'? It is like a soft power source'.

However, what distinguishes this comment from almost all other references to 'covering the stories others are not covering' is that it emphasises the importance of 'showing' that you care. As discussed in Chapter 3, the practice of reporting under-reported crises was almost always undertaken by humanitarian journalists to promote human equivalence, rather than to demonstrate to others that you care. We therefore conclude that while there is perhaps the potential for a unique form of symbolic capital to emerge – which combines both humanitarian and journalistic value – such capital does not currently circulate amongst the humanitarian journalists in our study. Furthermore, given that the presence of a unique form of symbolic capital is key to the establishment of a field (Fligstein and McAdam 2012), this provides further evidence to suggest that this social space is un-fielded.

Intermediary organisations

Social fields have 'internal governance units' (IGUs), such as trade associations and award committees, which help to legitimise and naturalise the logic and rules of the field (Fligstein and McAdam 2012). There were several non-profit 'intermediary' organisations that supported many of the journalists and news outlets in this space which could potentially serve a governance role as IGUs. Examples include the Pulitzer Centre on Crisis Reporting, GroundTruth, One World Media, the International Reporting Project, the International Women's Media Foundation and the Global Reporting Centre. These organisations do not directly produce content themselves. Rather, they channel donor funding into supporting international news either by awarding fellowships for individual journalists, by organising reporting trips to specific countries or occasionally, by providing support directly to news organisations. In doing to, they aim to act as a 'firewall' between journalists and donors: ensuring that editorial independence is maintained. As one intermediary representative put it,

> We are the 'middlemen'. We can make a very clean divide between where the money is coming from and who is receiving the money... so there is absolutely no chance that [journalists] would be able to bias their reporting based on who was funding them.

While most journalistic intermediaries, such as the European Journalism Centre (EJC) and the JournalismFund, seek to support professional journalism in general, these internationally focused intermediaries aim specifically to promote coverage of 'under-reported' international issues, by filling perceived 'gaps' in mainstream international news coverage. In this respect, they appear to share some of the norms and values held by humanitarian journalists. For example, in the following quotation from the director of one of these organisations, there is evidence of both an ambition to support coverage of under-reported issues and to add value to existing news coverage.

> Even from the beginning, it was intended that we were going to look at different issues all over the world, but with the idea of covering stories that were not being covered or perspectives that were not appearing in the major news outlet... We found ourselves

working with national outlets, with the same purpose of getting different perspectives or widening the lens with which they were covering the world; filling in the gaps.

It is also worth noting that, collectively, these journalistic intermediaries are responsible for supporting thousands of international news stories each year and for the career development of hundreds of international journalists. For example, before it closed in February 2018, the International Reporting Project had supported over 650 journalists to travel to 115 countries. As one intermediary representative put it, 'there is no question that we have a lot of leverage'. Another recently wrote that, 'today, it's a fair assumption that a handful of the international stories appearing daily in major outlets around the globe are made possible by fellowships'. These journalistic intermediaries also have an important influence on the particular social space occupied by humanitarian journalists. Many of the humanitarian journalists in our study had previously been funded directly by an intermediary and/or had worked for (or were currently working for) a news organisation which received money via one of these intermediaries.

Given their apparent influence and similar norms, it is reasonable to suggest that these intermediaries served as IGUs or 'catalyst actors' within the social space humanitarian journalists occupy because, by deciding which journalists and news outlets to support, and not support, they appear to be able to help govern the logic and rules operating in this space. Put simply, they can determine, to an extent, which humanitarian journalists are able to continue their professional practices, and which cannot.

However, there are several reasons to challenge this interpretation. First, the only criteria these intermediaries usually imposed upon journalistic grantees was either thematic or geographic. For example, the Pulitzer Centre had calls for proposals for international reporting projects on Religion and Peacebuilding, Religion and the Environment and on tropical rainforests in Latin America, Africa and Asia, while the International Reporting Project ran reporting trips to Lebanon, Nigeria, Uganda, Kenya, Liberia, Zambia and Ethiopia. As a result, these intermediaries generally did not dictate the particular professional practices their grantees adopted, or govern *how* journalists covered events. Moreover, despite appearing to share some similar professional norms and values with humanitarian journalists, these intermediaries' extended support to any professional journalists who wanted to report on 'under-reported' international stories. In fact, some of the criteria and measures of 'quality' and 'track record' these intermediaries imposed may have inadvertently disadvantaged humanitarian journalists, such as a need for significant reach amongst a 'mainstream' audience.

Second, these intermediaries were notably inconsistent in the criteria they each used to determine which journalists and news outlets to support. For example, unlike many other intermediaries, one of the key criteria for The Pulitzer Center was 'reach' – or having a distribution strategy that targeted relatively large news outlets. The outputs The Pulitzer Center supports also need to have a long 'shelf-life', so they remain relevant for their educational outreach projects for several years. This leads The Pulitzer Center to prioritise reporting projects that deal with longer-term, systemic issues, rather than breaking news. By contrast, other intermediaries, such as the International Women's Media Foundation, focus on addressing the lack of diversity in international news. Diversity here refers, not only to the range of places and issues being covered, but also to the kinds of people telling the stories. For example, one interviewee told us that they focus on 'broadening narratives from regions of the world that have been reported very narrowly and, historically also, through a white male gaze'. They went on to say that,

> We really believe that the people telling the story will bring their own experiences and tell stories in different ways... We very much believe that, when only white men are telling the story that we consume, that the stories are different than the ones that you would get if you had more people of colour and women telling stories.

In such cases, greater priority is given to supporting journalists from a wide variety of backgrounds, seeking to publish under-reported perspectives in a diverse range of publications in a range of countries. Such inconsistencies suggest that, even if these intermediaries were able to regulate the kinds of professional practices their grantees undertook, they would not be imposing any consistent logics or 'rules of the game'.

Finally, these intermediary organisations rarely engaged in any other field-building practices, aside from awarding financial support to journalists and lobbying a small group of largely philanthropic donors about the importance of international journalism in general, to secure funding. This contrasts clearly with, for example, the significant field-building activities undertaken by organisations such as the Global Investigative Journalism Network (GIJN) and the Solutions Journalism Network (SJN), in recent years, in the sub-fields of investigative journalism and solutions journalism. For example, the GIJN, which is an international association of non-profit investigative journalism organisations, provides training and networking opportunities for members, offers grants and fellowships, hosts an annual conference, administers an annual award and produces various resources such as a fortnightly bulletin, a 'help desk' and regular articles on 'member profiles' and 'tips and tools'. No such activities take place in the social space occupied by humanitarian journalists. There is no annual 'humanitarian journalism' conference, for instance.

The only potential exception to this is the relatively high profile One World Media Awards and ceremony, held annually by One World Media. These awards aim to 'recognise excellence in international journalism and filmmaking specifically from and about developing countries... celebrating those whose work brings to light underreported stories', within 15 different categories. However, it is difficult to interpret even these awards as an instance of field-building for humanitarian journalism because they are not seeking to reward any particular practices that are distinct from conventional journalism. Despite the use of the term 'under-reported', their focus is almost entirely geographic; 'on stories, topics or issues in, about or related to developing countries' and the different categories 'highlight work... across a wide range of genres and themes'. In this respect, their focus on supporting all international journalism about 'under-reported' events or topics suggests that they are too closely associated with the journalistic field to successfully advocate for a separate, discrete sub-field of humanitarian journalism. Given this, it appears there is currently an acute absence of 'internal governance units', or any kind of field-building activities, which could bring stability and order to a field of humanitarian journalism (Fligstein and McAdam 2012).

Conclusion

In this chapter, we examined whether humanitarian journalists occupy their own unique field. We argued that despite sharing some common professional practices, humanitarian journalists exhibit few other signs that would suggest the social space they occupy is fielded. Many of these individuals are not even aware of each other and those who are, are more likely to collaborate than compete. There is also little evidence of a shared identity, field-building actors, or a unique symbolic capital within this social space, which might help to sustain a field of 'humanitarian journalism'. Given this, we conclude that while it is possible that the field position occupied by humanitarian journalists may turn out to be a (very early) 'field-in-the-making' (Eyal and Pok 2011), it is currently best understood as a 'boundary zone' (Eyal 2013). We have also highlighted the differences between humanitarian journalists' norms and practices and those within seemingly similar news outlets, such as Al Jazeera English and the Thomson Reuters Foundation. Despite some potential similarities in some of their professional practices, the latter is far more competitive and institutionalised than the former.

References

Benson, R. and Neveu, E. (2005). *Bourdieu and the Journalistic Field.* Polity Press.

Eyal, G. (2013). Spaces between Fields. In Gorski, P. (Ed.), *Bourdieu and Historical Analysis.* Duke University Press. 158–182.

Eyal, G. and Pok, G. (2011). From a Sociology of Professions to a Sociology of Expertise. *Expert Determination Electronic Law Journal.* Retrieved from: http://expertdeterminationelectroniclawjournal.com/eyal-g-and-pok-g-2013-from-a-socio logy-of-professions-to-a-sociology-of-expertise/

Fligstein, N. and McAdam, M. (2012). *A Theory of Fields.* Oxford University Press.

Graves, L. and Konieczna, M. (2015). Sharing the News: Journalistic Collaboration as Field Repair. *International Journal of Communication.* 9. 1966–1984.

Heft, A. (2021). Transnational Journalism Networks "From Below". Cross-Border Journalistic Collaboration in Individualized Newswork. *Journalism Studies.* 22:4. 454–474.

Krause, M. (2014). *The Good Project: Humanitarian Relief NGOs and the Fragmentation of Reason.* University of Chicago Press.

Marchetti, D. (2005). Subfields of Specialised Journalism. In Benson, R. and Neveu, E. (Eds.), *Bourdieu and the Journalistic Field.* Polity Press.

Concluding remarks

Our ambition in this book has been to understand the work and practices of a small but important group of humanitarian journalists. In doing so, we sought to establish what viable alternatives there are to conventional journalistic approaches to reporting humanitarian affairs, which tend to produce selective, sporadic and formulaic coverage (Gutiérrez and García 2011; Kwak and An 2014; Ardèvol-Abreu 2016; Scott, Wright and Bunce 2018a). We found that a different kind of journalism is not only possible, it is being practiced. However, it also urgently needs support.

There are a small but important number of practicing humanitarian journalists working largely for specialist international news outlets – such as The New Humanitarian, Devex and HumAngle – who defy conventional journalistic norms. Instead, their practice is informed by a combination of journalistic and humanitarian values. Although these humanitarian journalists have a significant degree of freedom and flexibility in determining their practice – they share several key traits.

First, a combination of the humanitarian principle of moral equivalence and a journalistic concern for bearing witness leads them to minimise the news value of 'cultural proximity' in favour of 'reporting under-reported crises' (see Chapter 3). As a result, they focus on covering humanitarian crises that most other news outlets usually ignore. This is important because it can help to draw political and public attention towards neglected issues or under-funded humanitarian crises, as well as provide a potential 'early warning' for emerging crises (Olsen, Cartstensen and Hoyen 2002; van Belle, Rioux and Potter 2004; Hawkins 2008; Cohen, Riffe and Kim 2021; Ghanem 2022; Scott, Bunce and Wright 2022). It also provides content for mainstream news outlets to reference or re-publish if they would not have otherwise covered the story. More broadly, it begins to help challenge the 'hierarchy

DOI: 10.4324/9781003356806–7

of human life' that is so often reproduced by conventional news coverage of humanitarian affairs (Chouliaraki 2006; Joye 2009).

Second, the same combination of moral equivalence and bearing witness informs humanitarian journalists' sourcing practices (see Chapter 3). Rather than seeking primarily to 'humanise' a crisis or conform to a 'hierarchy of credibility' in their reporting, they focus instead on amplifying marginalised voices. Consequently, their coverage generally contains a more diverse range of sources including, not only affected citizens, but a range of other perspectives. This is important for many reasons. It can help to provide audiences with a more accurate picture of the realities on the ground and identify alternative ways of addressing an issue. This style of reporting can also help to challenge the dominant 'humanitarian imaginary', which foregrounds the perspectives of international actors (Calhoun 2010; Lawson 2021; Stupart 2022). In so doing, it can also present those connected to humanitarian affairs with more agency and dignity (Lugo-Ocando 2015; Lindner and Hartling 2018).

Third, humanitarian journalists tend to downplay the news value of 'immediacy' in favour of producing content that supplements or 'adds value' to mainstream news coverage (see Chapter 3). The concept of 'adding value' also resonates with both journalistic and humanitarian norms. This generally leads humanitarian journalists to publish longer-form, explanatory journalism rather than timelier, 'breaking news' coverage. This in-depth approach is important for supporting more informed humanitarian policymaking and action (Martin 2005; Franks 2013, 2015). It can also help engaged global audiences to better understand how and why crises happen (Philo 2002; Wright 2012; Imison 2013).

Forth, a combination of the humanitarian norms of neutrality and alleviating suffering – alongside the journalistic norm of impartiality – leads humanitarian journalists to adopt relatively outcome-oriented role perceptions – although they rejected the label of 'activists' (see Chapter 2). As a result, they generally aim to produce content that will ultimately 'make a difference' in some way, and/or that is solutions oriented. This approach can help citizens to understand what, if anything, they can do about distant crises – whether by pressuring politicians or supporting civil society organisations (Shaw 1996). For local communities and international humanitarian organisations, it can help provide new information and perspectives to support better decision-making (Ross 2004; Scott, Wright and Bunce 2018b).

Fifth, our respondents' understanding of the concept of 'humanitarianism' was more narrowly defined than the 'common-sense humanitarianism' adopted by most conventional journalists (and lay audiences) – though still more ambiguous than 'the humanitarianism of the professional humanitarians' (Tester 2010). As a result, humanitarian journalists tend to offer less sensationalist and more informed, qualified and accurate accounts of humanitarian affairs than conventional journalists (see Chapter 4). This not only supports their ambition to 'make a difference' through their reporting but also leads them to adopt more precise and appropriate terminology, which may be less stigmatising. However, this approach may also alienate less informed or engaged audiences (Cohen 2001).

Finally, their combined humanitarian and journalistic values also influenced humanitarian journalists' adoption of a watchdog function – albeit in a more complex way. Humanitarian journalists' outcome-oriented role perceptions and adherence to journalistic norms of promoting transparency and accountability do lead them to cover corruption, abuse and other failings within the humanitarian system. However, these influences are often in tension with the humanitarian principles of 'do no harm' and neutrality, and constrained by their often very limited resources and reliance on, and pursuit of, donor funding. In most cases, these competing influences generally resulted in the adoption of a constructive, rather than tenaciously critical watchdog function (see Chapter 2). However, their more in-depth understanding of the humanitarian system and humanitarian principles meant that their critical reporting was generally more informed than conventional journalism.

It is not our place to assess whether this constructive watchdog approach, and the various other features of humanitarian journalists' reporting are preferable to those of more conventional journalists. Such judgements depend on the normative underpinning of the criteria being used. Indeed, we argue below that such judgements also constitute 'boundary work', which may inadvertently undermine the potential for alternative, non-institutionalised practices to emerge. However, we do contend that a more diverse range of approaches to reporting on humanitarian affairs is preferable to one that is dominated almost exclusively by conventional journalistic approaches – whose limitations have been well documented (Cottle 2013; Nolan, Brookes and Imison 2020; Lawson 2021). Indeed, one of the key conclusions of Copper's (2020) analysis of the #aidtoo scandals in 2018 was that while they may have ultimately been exposed by legacy media, this was only possible because of their interaction with alternative media spaces such as WhatsApp and the Fifty Shades of Aid Facebook group.

Interestingly, few humanitarian journalists questioned the value of objectivity, impartiality and neutrality – likely because they are central to both the journalistic and humanitarian fields (Barnett 2011; Mellado 2021). However, these norms have been critiqued for constructing a false equivalence between different perspectives in situations of gross injustice, for example, and of helping to mask the influence of journalists own implicit worldviews (Wallace 2019). For this reason, Harb (2022) recently argued that 'it is time we see absolute objectivity, impartiality and neutrality is not always a prerequisite to quality journalism. In fact, when dealing with atrocities and human suffering they can be an obstacle in front of good, accurate, meaningful coverage'. Future research might therefore seek to document forms of humanitarian communication which do not depend on such principles, and which instead seek to be 'contextually objective', for example, by 'retaining their own sentiments, values and beliefs and their own audiences' sentiments, beliefs and values in mind when reporting' (Harb 2022).

Supporting humanitarian journalism: A tension

Unfortunately, despite offering a valuable compliment to conventional journalistic coverage of humanitarian affairs, humanitarian journalists are generally very precarious (see Chapter 2). The financial pressures that most journalists face are especially magnified for humanitarian journalists. This is because humanitarian affairs are one of the most expensive topics to report on, given challenges around access and safety. There are also very few audiences, advertisers or active donors willing to directly support such coverage. Furthermore, by eschewing conventional journalistic norms, humanitarian journalists may lose some of the status and credibility associated with the label of 'journalist', making it even more difficult to attract funding. This precarious financial situation affects their salaries, financial security and working conditions – and may also reduce diversity among journalists working in this space, as less well-off individuals may be less able to take financial risks. A relative lack of mainstream journalistic credibility can also undermine their audience reach, impact and access to sources – making it harder to do their job.

This financial and professional precarity also has implications for humanitarian journalists' autonomy because, in theory, marginalised actors are more vulnerable to donor capture (Benson and Neveu 2005). However, we showed that a combination of humanitarian and journalistic norms tends to lead to an emphasis on independence and political impartiality – meaning many humanitarian journalists strongly resisted any potential or perceived threats to their autonomy (see Chapter 2). For the same reason, the most active donors in this area are careful not to compromise, or been to seen compromise, their grantees' editorial independence (see Scott, Bunce and Wright 2019). Unfortunately, this combination of humanitarian journalists' defensiveness and donor's tentativeness can make it even harder to secure funding. This also helps to explain why there are so few humanitarian journalists.

Given the value of humanitarian journalism, and its counterpoint to conventional reporting, we argue that it needs greater support. Like other forms of journalism, any financial support offered should be transparent, reliable and fully respect journalistic editorial independence (Padania 2018). In Chapter 5, we suggested that journalistic intermediary organisations with similar norms and values, such as the Pulitzer Centre on Crisis Reporting and One World Media, may be one way of providing such support. However, efforts to support humanitarian journalists must be aware of an important tension: strengthening their professional standing may inadvertently undermine some of the defining aspects of their practice. For instance, humanitarian journalists currently have a relative freedom, which they value greatly, to determine their own professional practices, because they choose to operate in a space where professional norms are relatively un-regulated (see Chapter 3). However, such diversity and flexibility would be compromised if external support contributes to field-building activities that begin to determine which practices are more highly valued or how humanitarian journalists *should* behave. Even by writing this book, we have contributed to 'fielding' this space by introduced the label 'humanitarian journalists' and describing the common practices which typify their work. Similarly, humanitarian journalists collaborate, rather than compete, partly because they do not see themselves as seeking the same kinds of resources, occupying the same social space, or even sharing similar identities (see Chapter 5). This would likely change if 'humanitarian journalism' became more formally institutionalised because it would strengthen both the social hierarchies and the incentives to compete.

The main implication of this tension is certainly not that humanitarian journalists shouldn't be supported. Rather, it is that any efforts to support humanitarian journalists should be determined in partnership with humanitarian journalists themselves and the communities they serve. It is not for governments or private foundations to determine whether 'humanitarian journalism' should constitute a field, for example, or what practices should be most valued within it. Equally, private foundations and government donors should recognise that although their decisions over which actors to support may often be driven, in part, by logistical considerations – they also have important implications for the professional space they are funding (see Scott, Bunce and Wright 2019). Those intermediary organisations which already channel financial support to humanitarian journalists have an especially important role to play in determining if and how humanitarian journalism remains a 'boundary zone' between fields or becomes a 'field-in-the-making'. Their funding criteria, and decisions to undertake field-building activities, or not, are central to legitimating and naturalising the logic of an emergent field by determining which individuals and news outlets are able to continue their practices, and which are not (see Chapter 5).

Beyond news beats

In reaching these conclusions, we have found the work of Eyal (2006, 2013) and Eyal and Pok (2011) invaluable. They argue that if we only pay attention to professional practices that are firmly institutionalised, or which take place inside professional fields – such as journalism and humanitarianism – then we overlook a vast range of important alternative practices taking place at the 'boundary zone' between these fields. Humanitarian journalism is, we have shown, one such practice – alongside those of think tanks (Medvetz 2012), terrorism studies (Stampnitzky 2008), pole studios (Fennell 2018), alternative medicine (Lee 2004) and many more which have not yet been studied.

Furthermore, we have found many of the features of such 'boundary zones', which Eyal and Pok (2011) identify, key to explaining humanitarian journalists' professional practices. For example, their suggestion that acts of professional distinction, or 'boundary work', take place at the site of the boundary itself helps to explain why humanitarian journalists' professional identities are characterised by comparison with others – especially 'mainstream journalists' (see Chapter 2). Similarly, their proposal that such boundary work simultaneously connects and separates fields was borne out in our analysis of humanitarian journalists' descriptions of themselves as both journalists but not mainstream journalists, and as humanitarians but 'more objective' than aid agency communicators (see Chapter 2).

Furthermore, the idea that the boundary zone between fields serves as an under-regulated, 'space of opportunity' where actors are under less obligation to conform to the doxa of the field helps explains why humanitarian journalists have such freedom and flexibility in their practice (see Chapter 3). Eyal's (2013) suggestion that such liminal spaces allow for hybrid combinations of values from multiple different fields, explains why our respondents' practices are informed by both journalistic and humanitarian norms (see Chapter 3). The idea that a degree of definitional vagueness is necessary for ensuring that boundary zones remain 'spaces of opportunity' helps to explain why humanitarian journalists' understanding of 'humanitarianism' was broader and more ambiguous than that of 'professional humanitarians' (see Chapter 4). Finally, Eyal's (2013) distinction between a field, a field-in-the-making and a boundary zone between fields enabled us to distinguish between the professional practices of humanitarian journalists and those that remain within the journalistic field, such as those associated with different forms of 'ethically corrective journalism' (Berglez 2013) such as peace journalism (Galtung 2003) and counter-hegemonic journalism (Painter 2008) (see Chapters 1 and 5). It also drew our attention to the lack of common identity and field-building actors within the 'weakly institutionalised' social space occupied by our respondents (see Chapter 5).

This validation of much of Eyal (2006, 2013) and Eyal and Pok's (2011) conceptual framework invites us to question several common features of journalism studies. First, it invites us to ask – what are the unintended consequences of the common practice, within journalism studies, of policing the journalistic boundary ourselves – or of setting out parameters for deciding what does or should constitute 'journalism'? While such boundary work can help to exclude deviant actors seeking to claim the label of 'journalists' – it can also inadvertently obscure and undermine the possibility for other social significant practices to emerge within the periphery of the journalistic field.

Second, our analysis suggests that we regard the boundaries of journalism (and other social fields) as having the capacity to not only expand and contract – or be strengthened and weakened – but to have volume themselves, which can be occupied by professional actors. On this basis, we should ask – what other, yet unidentified, professional practices are taking place at the boundary zones between journalism and adjacent fields, such as sport, religion, politics and business? This may also invite us to re-assess the concept of a journalistic 'beat' and ask – when and why specialised subject areas of coverage might compromise 'boundary zones' between fields, where professional practices are characterised by boundary work, flexibility and strategic ambiguity? As one of our respondents explained,

> I have found this all over journalism: that journalists tend to end up looking a little bit like the beat they cover. If you are a diplomatic

journalist, you are quite sophisticated. And, if you cover the development sector, you tend to look at it like an aid worker – so you are egalitarian, you are cosmopolitan, you are do-goody.

Finally, when analysing journalistic 'beats', we might therefore begin to ask a new set of questions. Rather than focusing only on the degree of political control or economic dependence of a journalistic specialisation on the profession they cover – we should also ask what creative professional practices might be emerging because of hybrid journalistic and non-journalistic norms? Can they help us to re-imagine a more diverse set of approaches for communicating about important social issues, as humanitarian journalists do? In what way, for example, are the norms of the business world internalised and utilised by business journalists in their reporting? And what value do such practices hold?

The blind spots in a boundary zone

Despite its utility, Eyal (2006, 2013) and Eyal and Pok's (2011) conceptual framework is not without its own blind spots. In his account, Eyal (2013:170) strongly emphasises the advantages of occupying a boundary zone – describing marginality as, 'the mother of invention and improvisation' because it provides actors with a degree of freedom to experiment with hybrid professional practices. In fact, at one stage, Eyal (2013:180) even arguing that 'typically, the prizes to be had in the space between fields are relatively large – government money, media fame, connections'. He goes on to argue that, given these apparently 'high states' and their lack of regulation, boundary zones may be valuable for actors in other fields, because they provide them with the opportunity for 'raids'. Eyal (2013:180) defines 'raids' as an,

> incursion through blurred and penetrable boundaries, rapid amassing of profits in an under-regulated space with high stakes, and no less rapid retreat into one's original field where these profits may be reconverted into currency that will improve one's formerly marginal position within it.

We found no evidence of either 'high stakes' or 'raids' in the boundary zone between the fields of journalism and humanitarianism. Instead, our research consistently highlighted the high price that actors must pay for inhabiting this 'space of opportunity'. Being positioned far away from the autonomous pole within a field keeps them at a distance from the symbolic and material benefits this brings, with direct implications for their professional practice. Although our respondents, by definition, felt this was a price worth paying, this was because they valued their flexible professional practices very highly – not because they sought to return to another field with any 'rapidly amassed profits' (Eyal 2013:180). For this reason, we argue that Eyal (2013) understates how boundary zones serve as spaces of *precarity*. He also fails to explain how a boundary zone could retain 'high stakes' without quickly becoming fielded.

Eyal and Pok (2011) also focus exclusively on the professional practices of the actors working at the boundary zone. But what of the actors who choose to fund these practices, despite their peripheral position? What might they gain from supporting precarious, experimental practices that deviate from conventional, institutionalised norms? How should we understand their influence in determining which 'boundary zones' emerge into discrete fields of their own and which remain liminal, marginal practices – and the wider effects of such field building – especially given the relative vulnerability of actors at the boundary zone? For example, might those who support 'spaces of opportunity' at the boundaries of the journalistic field have an oversized impact on how the field of journalism evolves in future? In short, Eyal and Pok's (2011) framework currently obscures a focus on boundary zones as potential spaces of *co-option*.

Finally, what happens within a boundary zone is supposed to reveal the changing status of the respective fields within the wider field of power (Benson and Neveu 2005). For example, according to Medvetz (2012), the growth of think tanks within the US helps to reveal the changing social relations among power holders in the United States, or which forms of power will be considered the most legitimate and valuable in American society. Given the general lack of support for humanitarian journalists from both the fields of journalism and humanitarianism, our study suggests that neither field is growing significantly in terms of its 'importance to power holders' (ibid). But what our study does suggest is that despite this, there are individuals willing to sacrifice financial security to create new professional practices. In doing so, they show us that other ways of communicating about humanitarian affairs are possible.

References

Ardèvol-Abreu, A. (2016). The Framing of Humanitarian Crises in the Spanish Media: An Inductive Approach. *Revista Española de Investigaciones Sociológicas*. 155. 37–54.

Barnett, M. (2011). *Empire of Humanity: A History of Humanitarianism*. Cornell University Press.

Benson, R. and Neveu, E. (2005). *Bourdieu and the Journalistic Field*. Polity Press.

Berglez, P. (2013). *Global Journalism: Theory and Practice*. Peter Lang.

Calhoun, C. (2010). *The Idea of Emergency: Humanitarian Action and Global (Dis)Order*. Zone Books.

Chouliaraki, L. (2006). *The Spectatorship of Suffering*. Sage Publications.

Cohen, S. (2001). *States of Denial: Knowing about Atrocities and Suffering*. Polity and Blackwell Publishers.

Cohen, M. S., Riffe, D. and Kim, S. (2021). Media and Money: A 50 Year Analysis of International News Coverage and US Foreign Aid. *The Journal of International Communication*. 27:2. 172–191.

Cooper, G. (2020). #AidToo: Social Media Spaces and the Transformation of the Reporting of Aid Scandals in 2018. *Journalism Practice*. 15:6. 747–766.

Cottle, S. (2013). Journalists Witnessing Disaster: From the Calculus of Death to the Injunction to Care. *Journalism Studies*. 14:2. 232–248.

Eyal, G. (2006). *The Disenchantment of the Orient: Expertise in Arab Affairs and the Israeli State*. Stanford University Press.

Eyal, G. (2013). Spaces between Fields. In Gorski, P. (Ed.), *Bourdieu and Historical Analysis*. Duke University Press. 158–182.

Eyal, G. and Pok, G. (2011). From a Sociology of Professions to a Sociology of Expertise. *Expert Determination Electronic Law Journal*. Retrieved from: http://expertdeterminationelectroniclawjournal.com/eyal-g-and-pok-g-2013-from-a-socio logy-of-professions-to-a-sociology-of-expertise/

Fennell, D. (2018). Pole Studios as Spaces Between the Adult Entertainment, Art, Fitness and Sporting Fields. *Sport and Society*. 21:12. 1957–1973.

Franks, S. (2013). *Reporting Disasters: Famine, Aid, Politics and the Media*. Hurst Publishers.

Franks, S. (2015). From Pictures to Policy: How Does Humanitarian Reporting Have an Influence? In Cottle, S. and Cooper, G. (Eds.), *Humanitarianism, Communications and Change*. Peter Lang. 153–166.

Galtung, J. (2003). Peace Journalism. *Media Asia*. 30:3. 177–180.

Ghanem, Y. (2022). *Al Jazeera, Freedom of the Press, and Forecasting Humanitarian Emergencies*. Routledge.

Gutiérrez, J. and García, R. (2011). Assessing the Humanitarian Framing of the Spanish Press Coverage of the Darfur Crisis. *Ecquid Novi: African Journalism Studies*. 32:1. 66–81.

Harb, Z. (2022). Ukraine War: Is Impartiality Always Key to Quality Journalism? Al Jazeera English. Opinion. First published and accessed on 9 March 2022. https://www.aljazeera.com/opinions/2022/3/9/is-absolute-impartiality-always-a-necessity-in-journalism

Hawkins, V. (2008). *Stealth Conflicts: How the World's Worst Violence Is Ignored*. Ashgate.

Imison, M. (2013). '…A Story That's Got All the Right Elements': Australian Media Audiences Talk about the Coverage of a Health-Related Story from the Developing World. Communication, Politics and Culture.

Joye, S. (2009). The Hierarchy of Global Suffering. *The Journal of International Communication*. 15:2. 45–61.

Kwak, H. and An, J. (2014). *Understanding News Geography and Major Determinants of Global News Coverage of Disasters.* Computation and Journalism Symposium '14, New York.

Lawson, B. T. (2021). Hiding Behind Databases, Institutions and Actors: How Journalists Use Statistics in Reporting Humanitarian Crises. *Journalism Practice*. https://doi.org/10.1080/17512786.2021.1930106

Lee, J. (2004). Investigating the Hybridity of 'Wellness' Practices. Theory and Research in Comparative Social Analysis.

Lindner, E. G. and Hartling, L. (2018). Dignity in Times of Crises: Communicating the Need for Global Social Climate Change. In Anderson, R. and de Silva, P. L. (Eds.), *The Routledge Companion to Media and Humanitarian Action*. Routledge. 45–60.

Lugo-Ocando, J. (Ed.). (2015). *Blaming the Victim: How Global Journalism Fails Those in Poverty*. Pluto Press.

Martin, E. (2005). The Impact of the News Media in Shaping Canadian Development Assistance Policy. *Undercurrent*. 2:2. 28–40.

Medvetz, T. (2012). *Think Tanks in America*. University of Chicago Press.

Mellado, C. (Ed.). (2021). *Beyond Journalistic Norms: Role Performance and News in Comparative Perspective*. Routledge.

Nolan, D., Brookes, S. and Imison, M. (2020). Abandoning Either/Ors in Analyzing Shifts in Humanitarian Reporting. *Journalism Practice*. 14:1. 17–33.

Olsen, G. R., Cartstensen, N. and Hoyen, K. (2002). Humanitarian Crises: What Determines the Level of Emergency Assistance? – Media Coverage, Donor Interests and the Aid Business. In *Forgotten Humanitarian Crises. Conference on the Role of the Media, Decision-Makers and Humanitarian Agencies* [Conference Papers]. October 23, 2002. Copenhagen, Denmark.

Padania, S. (2018). *An Introduction to Funding Journalism and Media*. Ariadne Network and Transparency and Accountability Initiative.

Painter, J. (2008). *Counter-Hegemonic News: A Case Study of Al-Jazeera English and Telesûr*. Reuters Institute for the Study of Journalism. University of Oxford.

Philo, G. (2002). Television News and Audience Understanding of War, Conflict and Disaster. *Journalism Studies*. 3:2. 173–186.

Ross, S. (2004). *Toward New Understandings: Journalists and Humanitarian Relief Coverage*. Fritz Institute.

Scott, M., Bunce, M. and Wright, K. (2019). Foundation Funding and the Boundaries of Journalism. *Journalism Studies*. 20:14. 2034–2052.

Scott, M., Bunce, M. and Wright, K. (2022). The Influence of News Coverage on Humanitarian Aid: The Bureaucrats' Perspective. *Journalism Studies*. 23:2. 167–186.

Scott, M., Wright, K. and Bunce, M. (2018a). *The State of Humanitarian Journalism*. University of East Anglia.

Scott, M., Wright, K. and Bunce, M. (2018b). *Attitudes Towards Humanitarian News within the Aid Sector*. University of East Anglia. City, University of London.

Shaw, M. (1996). *Civil society and media in global crises: Representing distant violence*. Pinter Publishers Ltd.

Stampnitzky, L. (2008). *Disciplining Terrorism: How Experts Invented Terrorism*. Cambridge University Press.

Stupart, R. (2022). Forgotten Conflicts: Journalists and the Humanitarian Imaginary. In Chouliaraki, L. and Vestergaard, A. (Eds.), *The Routledge Handbook of Humanitarian Communication*. Routledge.

Tester, K. (2010). *Humanitarianism and Modern Culture*. Penn State University Press.

van Belle, D., Rioux, J. -S. and Potter, D. (2004). *Media, Bureaucracies and Foreign Aid*. Palgrave MacMillan.

Wallace, L. R. (2019). *The View from Somewhere: Undoing the Myth of Journalistic Objectivity*. University of Chicago Press.

Wright, K. (2012). Listening to Suffering: What Does Proper Distance Have to Do with Radio News? *Journalism*. 13:3. 284–302.

Index

Note: **Bold** page numbers refer to tables; *italic* page numbers refer to figures and page numbers followed by "n" denote endnotes.

For Product Safety Concerns and Information please contact our EU
representative GPSR@taylorandfrancis.com
Taylor & Francis Verlag GmbH, Kaufingerstraße 24, 80331 München, Germany

www.ingramcontent.com/pod-product-compliance
Lightning Source LLC
Chambersburg PA
CBHW061748270326
41928CB00011B/2415